Idaho

Pictorial Research by Arthur A. Hart

"Partners in Progress" by John Corlett, with J. Howard Moon, Carole Simon-Smolinski, and David Crowder

Introduction by Governor John V. Evans

Produced in cooperation with the Idaho State Historical Society

Windsor Publications, Inc.
Northridge, California

Facing page: *This hand-colored lithograph of the Shoshone Falls of the Snake River is dated circa 1850. Courtesy, Amon Carter Museum, Fort Worth*

Idaho

GEM OF THE MOUNTAINS

MERLE WELLS AND ARTHUR A. HART

To John Caylor

Windsor Publications, Inc.—History Book Division

Publisher: John M. Phillips
Editorial Director: Teri Davis Greenberg
Design Director: Alexander D'Anca

Staff for *Idaho: Gem of the Mountains*
Senior Editor: Julie Jaskol
Director, Corporate Biographies: Karen Story
Assistant Director, Corporate Biographies: Phyllis Gray
Editor, Corporate Biographies: Judith Hunter
Proofreader: Gail Koffman
Editorial Assistants: Lonnie Pham, Patricia Cobb, Pat Pittman, Kathy
   M. Brown, and Deena Tucker
Designer: Alexander D'Anca
Layout Artist: Ellen Ifrah

Library of Congress Cataloging in Publication Data

Wells, Merle W.
   Idaho, gem of the mountains.
   "Produced in cooperation with the Idaho State Historical Society."
   Bibliography: p. 248
   Includes index.
   1. Idaho—History. 2. Idaho—Description and travel. 3. Idaho—In-
dustries. I. Hart, Arthur A. II. Title.
F746.W43   1985   979.6   85-6384
ISBN 0-89781-141-0

ADVISORY COMMITTEE

Windsor Publications and the Idaho State Historical Society wish to
thank the following people for their valuable assistance in the prepara-
tion of this book:

John V. Evans	William D. Baker	John B. Fery	John H. Keiser	J.R. Simplot
David Leroy	Bethine Church	Thomas C. Frye	Carl C. Moore	Pete Thompson
James A. McClure	Arthur H. De Rosier, Jr.	Richard D. Gibb	Arthur C. Porter	Betty Penson Ward
A.L. Alford, Jr.	Curtis T. Eaton	J. Allen Jensen	Jim Siddoway	

These fun-loving University of Idaho students obviously enjoyed posing for this "deadpan" photo. The group styled itself "The Vegetarians." Courtesy, Idaho State Historical Society (ISHS)

Frederic B. Remington, painter of the American Old West, depicted Idaho's Register Rock, circa 1891. Courtesy, Amon Carter Museum, Fort Worth

Contents

of Indian lands, in 1805. Earlier expeditions across Mexico and Canada had left a broad unexplored zone in between. Lewis and Clark penetrated Rocky Mountain and Columbia River terrain in the hope they could ascend a navigable Missouri River tributary to an upper Columbia stream. Instead, they discovered a vast central Idaho mountain barrier that proved to be the most difficult obstacle in their entire trip. Although they barely managed to get past Idaho's rugged terrain they established friendly relationships with Shoshoni and Nez Perce Indian bands. Sacajawea, their Shoshoni interpreter who proved to be especially valuable in obtaining horses and essential assistance from her Lemhi people, eventually became Idaho's best-known woman.

Even with Sacajawea's help, Lewis and Clark ended up proving that their Missouri-Columbia river navigation scheme simply would not work. Clark explored a difficult stretch of Salmon River gorge only to learn that he could not get through Idaho's mountains there. His Shoshoni guide informed him that:

the Mountains Close and is a perpendicular Clift on each Side, and Continues for a great distance and that the water runs with great violence from one rock to another on each Side foaming & roreing thro rocks in every direction, so as to render the passage of any thing impossible. Those rapids which I had seen he said was Small & trifeling in comparison to the rocks & rapids below, at no great distance & The Hills or mountains were not like those I had seen but like the side of a tree straight up.

Since they could not proceed with canoes, Lewis and Clark had to use a rough mountain ridge trail. Clark reported a great deal of trouble in commencing that passage:

We ... proceeded ... over Steep points rockey & buschey as usual for 4 miles to an old Indian fishing place, here the road leaves the river to the left and assends a mountain winding in every direction to get up the Steep assents & to pass the emence quantity of falling timber ... the party came up much fatigued & horses more so, several horses Slipped and rolled down Steep hills. ...

Within two years, however, Canadian fur traders found a practical way to get through Idaho's northern mountain barrier, and beaver trappers went to work along streams that Lewis and

Left: When Lewis and Clark crossed what would later be known as Idaho, they carried "peace medals" like this one for presentation to Indian leaders. They showed President Thomas Jefferson in profile on one side and the clasped hands of a soldier and an Indian on the other. This example is in the Idaho Historical Museum at Boise. (ISHS)

Right: The fur trade in Idaho began with the establishment of David Thompson's Kullyspel House on Lake Pend d'Oreille. This 1950 view by Ross Hall shows tiny Mamaloose Island, center, and the slender peninsula leading toward it where Thompson built his post. Today the lake is noted for its beauty and its excellent fishing. Courtesy, Ross Hall

Facing page, top: President Thomas Jefferson invited his young Virginia neighbor Meriwether Lewis to be his private secretary in 1801. In 1803 he named Lewis co-leader of an expedition to explore the newly acquired Louisiana Purchase. This best-known likeness of Meriwether Lewis was painted by Charles Willson Peale. Courtesy, Library of Congress

Facing page, bottom: William Clark met Meriwether Lewis on a frontier Indian campaign in Kentucky. They became good friends, leading to Lewis' invitation to Clark to join him as co-leader of the expedition that made them both famous. Clark served as governor of Missouri Territory from 1813 to 1821. Courtesy, Library of Congress

Clark had missed.

Coming south from his British Columbia fur trade post in 1808, David Thompson, an English surveyor and geographer, discovered a practical way to get through North Idaho. A successful North West Company field commander of Canadian trappers, he started Idaho's initial fur trade as part of a vast beaver empire based in Montreal. In 1809 he built an Idaho post on Lake Pend d'Oreille and extended his operation into northwestern Montana. Andrew Henry, responsible for upper Missouri's fur trade, countered with an expedition of fur hunters from St. Louis. Fleeing from Montana's Blackfoot Indians, his trappers built a temporary southeastern Idaho post in 1810. New York financier John Jacob Astor also competed for Idaho furs.

In 1811, Astor's associate, Wilson Price Hunt, and Donald Mackenzie, who established most of Idaho's fur trade, led a Pacific Fur Company overland expedition to Astor's new base in Oregon, exploring southern Idaho's sagebrush plains on their way. After trying to descend an impassable Snake River gorge above Twin Falls in canoes, they had to walk to Astoria, Oregon, a winter hike of more than 800 miles. In 1812 prominent fur trader Robert Stuart's party returning to St. Louis from Astoria found a satisfactory south pass in Wyoming, a route for overland travel from St. Louis that had eluded Lewis and Clark. By that time, Astor's Pacific Fur Company had failed, and the Wyoming route was eventually used by emigrants of the Oregon Trail.

Impressed with Idaho's beaver resources, Mackenzie returned west in 1816 to organize a new Snake country fur trade venture in eastern Washington. In 1818 he expanded his operations into Idaho, which he continued to explore. Hudson's Bay Company fur-hunting brigades, which took over Mackenzie's North West Company, trapped along Idaho streams until 1834. Fort Hall and Fort Boise were built by trappers as local bases for beaver-hunting operations.

After 1824 parties of mountain men based in St. Louis roamed

Above: *Fort Hall, the American fur trade post built by Nathaniel Wyeth of Boston in 1834, looked like this in 1849. (ISHS)*

Facing page, top: *Kit Carson was a legend in his own time. He trapped beaver throughout the West, gained a reputation for reckless bravery at rendezvous, and led John C. Fremont's expedition across Idaho to Oregon and California in 1843. (ISHS)*

Facing page, bottom: *Donald Mackenzie was one of the great explorers of early Idaho. His contemporaries labeled him "perpetual motion," and "King of the Northwest" for his astonishing energy and leadership ability. Mackenzie's 300-pound bulk did not slow him down; it only added to the impression he made wherever he went. (ISHS)*

through southern Idaho, competing with British and Canadian fur hunters for beaver until 1840. Two decidedly different groups of fur hunters trapped Idaho beaver after 1824. Powerful aristocratic leaders, following Donald Mackenzie's system, commanded Hudson's Bay Company brigades that continued to explore Idaho's beaver country. Hudson's Bay Company chief factor Peter Skene Ogden led six of these annual expeditions, going on to search for furs in later Nevada, Utah, Arizona, California, and Oregon. Under a strict company policy to avoid Indian hostilities, he competed, with considerable success, for what limited beaver resources were left in a land where no one had much incentive to practice conservation.

Ogden's rivals from St. Louis followed a different system. Individualistic and self-reliant, they also had to travel in hunting parties for protection. Most mountain men who traded with St. Louis companies in an annual summer trade fair resisted any kind of authoritarian control. They had a wild, free life far from most restraints imposed by conventional society of their time.

Idaho's 1824 Snake-area trappers included Jim Bridger, who went on to lead a series of Idaho trapping expeditions. Bridger participated in Rocky Mountain fur trade fairs along Bear Lake in 1826 and 1827 and in Pierre's Hole (later renamed Teton Valley) in 1829 and 1832. He regarded Pierre's Hole as "the best valley in the world," although in 1832 a battle with a Blackfoot band made it dangerous as well. Bridger also introduced other prominent mountain men to Idaho's fur trade, among them Kit Carson. Carson shifted to Thomas McKay's Hudson's Bay Company trappers for a season in 1836 but soon rejoined his Rocky Mountain colleagues. Captain B. L. E. Bonneville, an army officer on leave to do some exploring and fur hunting, also gained a great reputation in Idaho and other western areas. Although his 1832 to 1834 expeditions fared poorly as beaver enterprises, he is noted for publication of his *Adventures,* a literary narrative prepared by Washington Irving in 1836. By that time, silk hats were replacing beaver hats in the world of fashion, and low prices and declining demand brought the fur trade to an end.

Unlike settlers who later followed Idaho's emigrant roads, fur hunters traveled and lived much as Indian bands did, hunting for subsistence and moving along seasonal migratory routes. Some Idaho Indians were persuaded to go into fur hunting for Hudson's Bay Company traders, but many of them refused to pursue beaver, an occupation they regarded as totally absurd.

Right: *South Idaho mining camps of the nineteenth century flourished into boom towns—some to grow into modern cities, and others to decay as ghost towns. Courtesy, Don Watts*

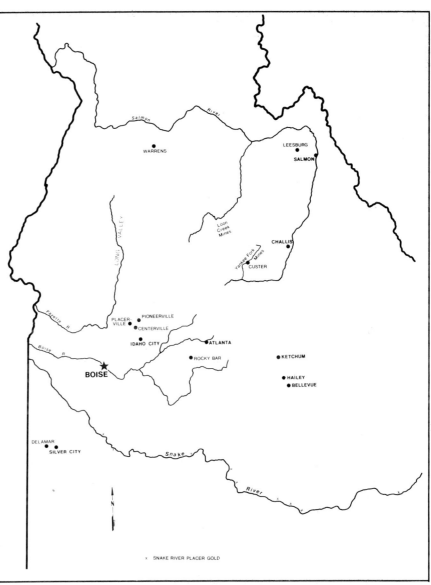

ho's population was settled near Boise.

When Idaho became a territory, provision had not been made for white acquisition of Indian lands. Arrangements had not been made for non-Indian settlement at all. Mining and farming were in violation of United States law, particularly around Pierce and Florence. Nez Perce Indians were angry about this massive invasion of the reservation lands guaranteed them by Congress in 1859. They threatened to divert the energy of Idaho's miners toward fighting rather than mining.

Soldiers from Fort Walla Walla were supposed to turn back all miners or settlers who wanted to enter Nez Perce territory, yet they had failed to evict Pierce City's founders in 1860. After that, Civil War distractions intervened to allow mining to go unchecked. By 1863, governmental and military authorities concluded that they would have to open most Nez Perce reservation lands to mining and settlement. Very few Indians would agree to relinquish their traditional territory, but the new treaty was concluded leaving Nez Perce bands with those Idaho lands not in demand for mining or ranching. From then on, Nez Perce Indians from Oregon and Washington, along with an important Idaho band camped below Florence, declined to enter into any more treaty commitments. Those who still inhabited reservation lands gained little or no benefit from their revised treaty after it went into effect in 1867. By that time, local gold rushes were over, but ranching and mining continued to interfere with Nez Perce life and traditions.

Southern Idaho's Indians fared no better. After 1862 when a host of Boise Basin miners invaded traditional Shoshoni lands, another large bloc of Indian country was settled by whites. A Northern Shoshoni treaty had not been negotiated for southwestern Idaho, although an arrangement for one was finally made in Boise in 1864.

Hostilities between settlers and Indians continued to afflict much of southern Idaho until 1867, when a reservation was established at Fort Hall in a traditional Shoshoni and Bannock area. In 1868 an Indian treaty covering southeastern Idaho (which no longer included Wyoming) took care of a large but unsettled domain. Two treaties that covered southwestern Idaho's mining country were never ratified and Indian land rights there remain unextinguished.

Indian land rights disregarded, a gold rush to Boise Basin attracted 40,000 miners or more from 1862 to 1864. Even after a large summer population had left, more than 16,000 remained in permanent camps primarily near Idaho City, Placerville, Centerville, and Pioneerville. Prospecting in neighboring mountains led to additional rich discoveries at Rocky Bar, Silver City, and Atlanta. North Idaho gained an important new camp at Warren in 1862, but for two decades most of Idaho's miners worked in southern Idaho.

An almost impassable mountain and canyon barrier separated Idaho's two mining regions, and until Idaho became a state in 1890 a great deal of effort was devoted to territorial boundary reform. North Idaho never managed to become part of a new territory or return to Washington (of which it had been a part for a decade before Idaho was established) but remained a minority section in a badly divided territory after 1862.

Facing page: Few stamp mills ever had the architectural quality of the Shoenbar mill at Silver City. This 1866 photograph shows it to have been a masterpiece of the stonemason's art. Stamp mills crushed gold- and silver-bearing rock into powder as a first step in extracting the precious metal. (ISHS)

Unlike Florence, Boise Basin had large areas of productive gold claims that could accommodate thousands of miners. When winter snows melted and water was available, placer operations continued day and night. Evenings in Idaho City presented a "grand view." T. J. Butler reported on April 30, 1864, that he:

counted more than thirty mining fires on Tuesday evening from a single standpoint in front of our Boise News *office door. The ringing of shovels as the auriferous gravel slides from the blade, is distinctly audible above the murmur of the water in the sluices, conspiring with the haze and smoke through which the mountains beyond are dimly visible to render the scene most interesting and lovely.*

Wages, as at Florence, were extremely high for those days—six dollars a day and seven dollars for night work. More than ten or fifteen times as much as miners in Pennsylvania had been getting not so long before, wages were high enough to be really attractive during each year's short mining season. Lucky claim

GOLD RUSH

Gold rushes continued in Idaho for a decade or two after 1864, when the initial sequence of major excitements at Florence and Boise Basin had ended. In 1866 a group of Montana miners found gold at Leesburg. That winter the fortune hunters almost starved, until a company of snow shovelers hacked a trail through twenty-foot drifts to get to the camp. Eight cattle that managed to get through a narrow channel to Leesburg, March 8, 1867, were certainly "a welcome sight to the denizens of this . . . isolated but rising town," according to a Montana newspaper correspondent.

Packers from Idaho City discovered rich placers in a rough mountain wilderness halfway along their route to Leesburg in 1869. Between August 14 and August 19, "miners, merchants, tradesmen, and excitement hunters" rushed to Loon Creek, deserting Idaho City, Centerville, Placerville, Granite Creek, Pioneer, and Boston.

Mining interest expanded in 1870 from Loon Creek to placers at nearby Yankee Fork. Operations there got off to a slow start until a highly productive lode named

for General George Armstrong Custer was located in 1876. By 1878 and 1879 a regular old-fashioned gold rush was attracting a host of miners to Bonanza and Custer, camps about two miles apart on Yankee Fork. A number of easily worked lodes around Custer became prominent even though they were in a remote location where mining was expensive. After 1939 Yankee Fork dredging projects raised gold production there from twelve to about fourteen million dollars.

Leesburg, a placer mining camp started in 1866, looked like this in 1974. Although the Civil War was over, the dominant Confederate faction in the new camp named it for Robert E. Lee. Northern miners started a rival camp next door called Grantsville, but the name was soon dropped in favor of Leesburg for the entire diggings. (ISHS)

These elegant croquet players certainly seem out of place in the rustic setting of an Idaho mining camp. Bonanza, in the Yankee Fork district, was a collection of log cabins and rough board shacks in the 1880s when this photo was taken. From the formality of the dress one can guess that it was a Sunday. (ISHS)

holders who worked for themselves often earned several times as much as highly paid miners received. Only a few made a really large fortune, but enough miners succeeded in setting themselves up in business or farming that one gold rush followed another.

In addition to placer operations, Boise Basin, Rocky Bar, and Silver City miners looked for gold and silver lodes. All stream deposits of gold originate as metal-bearing rock (generally quartz) that comes from fissures in mountain ridges. When mountains are worn down by stream erosion, gold from quartz lodes is deposited in gravel near bedrock, but remainders of gold lodes are often left under surface dirt that covers practically all hills and ridges. Prospectors set about panning samples from likely areas above placer deposits in search of the lodes from which they came. Outcrops of quartz veins were ground up and panned for gold. Prospectors who discovered rich samples tried to get investors to develop their lodes. Unlike many placer claims, lode properties required elaborate equipment, expensive underground tunnels and workings, and substantial industrial plants to grind up ore and recover precious metals. Major capital investment had to be found in order to operate a lode mine.

Financial resources to develop lode mines were provided in some camps by successful placer operations. Influential community leaders, often with legislative or judicial experience, brought in investment capital to augment local resources that were derived from early placers.

J. Marion More was as prominent as any of Idaho's early mining magnates. A Washington legislator who became a founder of Idaho City in 1862, he gained mining experience and interests in all parts of Idaho and developed major Owyhee silver lodes in addition to his Boise Basin holdings. A widely admired Irishman, More was noted for his "simple, frank and affectionate temperament, his generosity and manliness of character, and his entire freedom from narrow and sordid views. . . ." He impressed his associates with his "unceasing benevolence and charity" and integrity uncommon among mine developers of his time, according to *Idaho World*, April 8, 1868. Although he could not avoid the financial disasters that set back almost all early lode mining camps, More was able to surmount such obstacles when most other promoters and managers failed. When overexpansion, reckless management, and lack of capital forced his Silver City mines and mills to close for a time in 1867, More's forthright ex-

Above: *Dr. C.K. Ah Fong practiced medicine in Idaho mining camps from gold rush times. He was probably the best qualified doctor in the territory in those pioneer days, treating many white patients as well as Chinese. (ISHS)*

Left: *There were still a few Chinese miners working Idaho placers at the turn of the century. These men are operating a hydraulic giant at the Royal placer operation near Rocky Bar in about 1900. (ISHS)*

Facing page, top: *The tired face of young miner Fred Turner of Pearl, Idaho, poignantly suggests the hardships and dangers of hardrock mining. Turner had a wife and small children to support; the brutal work made him old before his time. Courtesy, Gem County Historical Society*

Facing page, bottom: *Many Chinese miners found other kinds of work when gold mining fizzled out. This man was a cook on an Idaho cattle ranch. Well-to-do Boise families also hired Chinese domestic help, as did hotels and restaurants on the frontier. (ISHS)*

planation and promise to improve his operation and pay off his company debts from his own funds won community sympathy and support. He was killed in a bitter Silver City mining claims war that required military intervention from Fort Boise, but his mining enterprises went on. Idaho City and Silver City retained their commercial and industrial importance.

A few bonanza areas gained a reputation for violence. Civil War hostilities affected western mining camps as well as southern borderlands. An assortment of bandits and Confederate refugees made a confused situation more complex in places where regular law enforcement was unavailable and government remained disorganized. Rocky Bar and Silver City had less trouble with the robberies that afflicted Boise Basin camps and Florence, but they suffered a series of mining claim wars.

Silver City's rich silver lodes brought on a series of armed conflicts between rival claimants. In 1865 a company of Poorman Mine claim jumpers managed to make off with about a half-million dollars of another company's silver in only one week's work before their operation could be shut down by a court injunction. In a similar Silver City claims war in 1868, private armies representing adjacent rival companies got into an armed conflict, both above ground and below. At a cost of about $40,000, that battle turned out to be about as expensive and destructive as earlier litigation over Poorman lode ownership had been. Other less spectacular claim wars were fought more in court, although Rocky Bar experienced episodes of violence similar to Silver City's troubles.

Idaho's early mining camps, particularly those with great

wealth, attracted all kinds of miners from many lands. Some nationalities congregated in particular camps. Pioneer City, for example, was noted as an Irish center. Other camps had a more varied population. When richer deposits were worked out, Chinese miners were allowed to come in to exploit placers too low-grade or difficult to interest anyone else. Chinese operators devised more effective recovery methods and labored for less pay than most white miners. By 1870, when most early placer camps had gone into decline, Idaho's typical miner was Chinese, and Idaho boasted more Chinese miners than any other western commonwealth.

Women and children were uncommon in a gold rush. Early placer camps were mostly transient in nature, and those located in remote mountain country offered little attraction to families. Florence, however, had a population large enough to justify a school for children. Idaho City and Placerville were also large permanent placer camps stable enough to encourage families to

Above: *Young Joseph had attained a national reputation as a "red Napoleon" when this engraved portrait was published in the 1880s. Although not the military leader his admirers thought, his noble bearing and statesmanlike surrender speech in 1877 made him famous. He continued to speak for justice for his people until his death in 1904. (ISHS)*

Top: *Joseph of the Nez Perce posed with pipe in hand, center, with others of his band for this photograph a few years before his death in 1904. The great leader commanded national respect and sympathy. (ISHS)*

Montana, where they traditionally hunted buffalo. They went on a ten-week expedition, punctuated by army attacks in Montana and southeastern Idaho that eventually drove most of the warriors to a temporary exile in Canada. Chief Joseph remained with those unfit for travel to Canada, negotiating with Howard for their return to Idaho. Instead the Nez Perce were forced into an eight-year confinement in Oklahoma.

Chief Joseph gained a national reputation as an Indian leader. During his eight-year campaign to get back to his Pacific Northwest homeland, he gave press interviews and wrote magazine articles articulately expressing his plight. Some of his people were eventually admitted back to Idaho, but Joseph and others of his Oregon associates had to go to northern Washington's Colville reservation.

Other Idaho Indians also had trouble with the overgrazing of their lands. Aside from supporting sheep and cattle herds, early Idaho rangelands—particularly areas along Goodale's Cutoff across Camas Prairie—provided forage for hog drives. Bannock Indians, who had reserved Camas Prairie along with their lands at Fort Hall, had great difficulty surviving when plains buffalo herds disappeared and other traditional sources of subsistence became unavailable. By 1878 Bannock opposition to cattle grazing and hog drives through Camas Prairie helped set off Idaho's last major Indian war. Moving west from their Camas grounds to join their Northern Paiute associates in Oregon, 100 to 200 disaffected Bannock soon were driven back to Idaho. Most wound up at Fort Hall, where confinement in the reservation ended forever their way of life.

As Native American objections to expanded agriculture were silenced, high local prices for farm and ranch products enabled Idaho's suppliers of mining camps to invest in modern machinery and develop lands faster than new frontier settlers ordinarily

Bearded John M. Ross home-steaded in the lower Boise Valley in 1864. When this family portrait was made in 1886, young Charles Benjamin, third from left, was ten years old. Idaho finally elected a native son governor in 1930, giving C. Ben Ross that honor. Most earlier Idaho governors were midwesterners. (ISHS)

could. Farms were established at a time when new, superior equipment was becoming available. By 1865 Peoria breaking plows were employed in Idaho to open new farmland, and huge harrows were available to prepare soil for planting. Boise Valley had seven threshing machines by 1870, and improved binders that did not require farmers to tie their sheaves of wheat followed within a decade. A variety of mowers, rakes, headers, and reapers became available, along with steam traction engines.

By 1877 H.P. Isaacs had imported modern Swiss porcelain rollers for his new-process flour mill, using a technology that supplanted mill stones. Cy Jacobs, another of Idaho's more prominent flour millers, also employed an efficient system in which he operated a distillery as well. He fed mash from his distillery to hogs which he used as a source for lard to supply his soap and candle factory. Eventually his mill ditch supplied electric power for a street car system. This kind of imaginative, integrated industrial development was employed in all parts of Idaho.

Lack of rail transportation helped early Idaho farmers and processors retain local markets without much competition from

CONTINUING INDIAN CLAIMS

About a century after miners and ranchers began to appropriate large tracts of Indian lands, Idaho's Nez Perce, Shoshoni, and Coeur d'Alene tribes were awarded payments to help compensate them for their losses. After years of litigation, Congress established an Indian Claims Commission in 1946. A variety of Idaho claims were argued and adjudicated before Congress appropriated additional compensation for lands acquired by Indian treaties and for royalties for gold mined illegally in Nez Perce territory between 1860 and 1867.

More than $30 million was paid to Idaho Indian claimants to cover treaties "that should be revised on the ground of fraud, duress, unconscionable consideration, mutual or unilateral mistake," or other dishonorable dealings. Except for southwestern Idaho, where a Boise and Bruneau Shoshoni claim had been filed in error for another tribe, all Nez Perce, Shoshoni, and Coeur d'Alene land treaties were reviewed and adjusted by 1971.

As a result of Senate failure to ratify treaties of 1864 and 1866, Congress never managed to obtain title to Boise and Bruneau lands at all. That oversight was never rectified by Indian Claims Commission review, and by 1984, Boise and Bruneau claimants still had not succeeded in obtaining congressional redress for a long series of blunders that left their land-ownership problem unrecognized and unsolved.

Aside from the Boise claim, Idaho's Indians have been able to make substantial gains in preserving their traditional independence and values after a century or more of pressure to abandon their tribal identity. Idaho's Indian population of 10,418 in 1980 approximated that of 1800, a remarkable achievement considering everything they had to overcome in order to survive as a people. Except for loss of a Pend d'Oreille or Flathead band to Montana in 1854, and the gain of a Delaware band that settled on an island north of New Plymouth in 1924, Idaho's organized tribes

of 1984 were identical to those of 1800. Urban Indians represented about a third of Idaho's total in 1980, with twice that number retaining their traditional tribal affiliation.

Prominent Idaho Indians began to enter state legislative service after 1956. Two were elected in 1984, when Indian interests were getting more legislative attention than they had received a generation earlier. Through their state inter-tribal council, Idaho's Indians developed an improved organization to present their views upon important issues, and although they still had major problems in asserting their treaty rights to water resources and to traditional hunting and fishing areas, they had advanced considerably on their way toward tribal autonomy and self-sufficiency.

Joseph R. Garry, great-great grandson of Spokane Garry, the nineteenth-century chief of the Spokane Indians, took up modern leadership of the Northwestern Indians. As president of the National Congress of American Indians and Idaho state senator, Garry referred to himself as a "legislative warrior." (ISHS)

Above: *This lithograph of Lake Pend d'Oreille, Idaho's biggest lake, appeared in Elliott's 1884 history. The Northern Pacific Railway had just completed the long wooden bridges and transcontinental trains could cross Idaho's northern panhandle. Sternwheel steamboats had operated on Pend d'Oreille since 1866. (ISHS)*

Right: *The hazards of railroading in winter are dramatically shown in this 1913 shot of a locomotive with a rotary snowplow forcing its way through twelve-foot drifts near Ashton. There was still plenty of manual shoveling to be done before trains could get through. (ISHS)*

Right, below: *Trains were sometimes snowbound in winter, despite the efforts of snowplows to keep mountain grades clear. This locomotive at Blackfoot in 1917 has just bucked its way through snowdrifts to get into town. (ISHS)*

Above: *The natives gathered quickly to view a fallen giant like this Oregon Short Line locomotive when it went off the tracks near Montpelier in about 1905. Few events this dramatic disturbed the tranquility of rural Idaho life, and everyone wanted a picture to preserve the memory. (ISHS)*

Right: *Big iron horses like these still pulled Union Pacific freight trains up steep Idaho grades in 1938 when this picture was taken near Bliss. "Helper" locomotives were added at stations along the way as needed. (ISHS)*

The Clark Sherwood family of Payette found the shade of a mountain aspen grove a delightful spot for a Fourth of July picnic. Although they are dressed in holiday best, it is easy to tell that the men are farmers from their deeply tanned faces and white fore-heads—foreheads protected in the fields by wide-brimmed straw hats. (ISHS)

remote suppliers. After 1880, when railroads began to reach more of Idaho's previously isolated farm communities, national commercial markets became available for specialized products such as potatoes.

Rail service essential for large-scale commercial farming finally reached Idaho's Palouse farms after Northern Pacific Railway builders crossed Idaho in 1881. Because of mountain obstacles and forbidding canyons, Northern Pacific route engineers had to detour through Spokane Valley to Rathdrum and Sandpoint. Moscow had a branch line within four more years, and other settlements eventually gained rail transportation, too. North Idaho finally had three transcontinental rail lines which together with a Canadian Pacific connection, served almost all important areas suitable for farm settlement.

Right: *A leather-aproned blacksmith surveys Weiser's Main Street in about 1888. A fire in 1890 would destroy all of the promise shown in this view, but the young supply center to valley farms and ranches would be rebuilt quickly, and more permanently. The 1890 fire started in the Weiser City Hotel. (ISHS)*

Below: *This young woman is delighted at the progress being made on her new log house in Idaho's mountains. Hundreds of settlers built cabins along the Salmon, Clearwater, and other rivers far from civilization. They lived by raising their own vegetables, grazing cattle, hunting, and fishing. (ISHS)*

Right: *The town band, excited little boys, and 170 union miners turned out for Silver City's 1898 Labor Day parade. Miners there had been organized into unions since 1867. (ISHS)*

Below: *Young Twin Falls welcomed two circuses in the summer of 1909. The elephants parading down Main Avenue in this colorful view were part of the Sells Floto circus of July 3. The Hagenbeck-Wallace Troupe played Twin Falls July 23, 1909. Note that the enterprising circus sold advertising space on the elephants' broad sides to local merchants. (ISHS)*

centers of commerce and industry, while others had optimistic ambitions that could not be realized for many years. Remote from major concentrations of population, and lacking oil fields, iron mines, and commercial coal deposits, Idaho did not develop large industrial cities. Opportunities for starting smaller model communities were attractive, though. These ranged from carefully designed farm centers to company towns of mining and logging enterprises.

Almost all of Idaho's well-planned agricultural towns were Mormon. Wide streets, substantial mansions, landmark tabernacles, and other ornate church structures distinguished Mormon towns from other communities. Montpelier, a Mormon village of 1864 that gained a railroad center after 1880, developed a contrasting display of both varieties of urban design. A business district constructed by anti-Mormon planners, featuring narrow streets and railroad structures, displaced part of an earlier Mormon grid. Most Mormon towns, however, escaped that kind of redevelopment and retained their traditional design.

These young citizens of Kellogg enjoyed a popular winter sport in early Idaho—a ride in a one-horse open sleigh. The "cutter," as it was called, was a graceful, strong, and lightweight vehicle that skimmed through the streets to the accompaniment of jingling sleigh-bells. (ISHS)

A somewhat different effort at community planning was undertaken in southwestern Idaho. New Plymouth grew out of a plan developed in 1894 in Boston, where author and orator Edward Everett Hale helped William E. Smythe, president of the National Irrigation Congress, elicit interest and support for organizing a model cooperative colony. Settlers, primarily with professional, business, or industrial experience, came mainly from Chicago and Cleveland. Each colonist subscribed to twenty

Livery stables like this one in Lewiston's Liberty Theater building continued in operation well into the twentieth century. Ike Binnard was proud of his handsome black horse and his rubber-tired spring buggy in this 1912 photo. Courtesy, Lewiston Tribune

shares of stock in a development company and received twenty acres of irrigated orchard or farmland. Smythe reported in 1899 upon their enthusiasm and success in clearing sagebrush and starting a new, decidedly different way of life:

The Plymouth industrial programme aimed at complete economic independence of the people by the simple method of producing the variety of things consumed, on small, diversified farms; of having surplus products, principally fruit, for sale in home and eastern markets; and by combining the capital of the settlers, by incorporation of a stock company, to own and develop the town-site, and to erect and operate simple industries required in connection with products of the soil. On the social side the plan aimed to give these farmers the best advantages of town life, or at least of neighborhood association. This was accomplished by assembling the houses in a central village, laid out, in accordance with a beautiful plan, with residences grouped on an outside circle touching the farm at all points. This

plan brought the settlers close together on acre-lot—"home acres"—thus preventing isolation, and giving them the benefits of school, church, post-office, store, library, and entertainments.

The Plymouth settlers have been contented and prosperous from the first, and have had less than the usual share of early trials and disappointments. They testify that the social advantages of the colony plan, as compared with the drawbacks of individual and isolated settlement, are alone sufficient to warrant its use.

By 1900 about 280 settlers had arrived. That population remained constant for a decade, but grew to over a thousand by 1980.

In contrast to places like New Plymouth, a substantial number of Idaho communities strove for ascendancy in their regions as large population centers. Lewiston and Moscow grew into rivals for commercial supremacy in an area south of Spokane. Lewiston had to wait until 1898 for rail connections that had been available in Moscow more than a decade before. Moscow already dominated a nationally important wheat-producing area that extended from eastern Washington into Idaho. But with access to an enlarged Camas Prairie agricultural area after 1894, when Nez Perce Indians agreed to sale of reservation lands to white farmers, Lewiston was able to grow more rapidly.

Moscow's ascendency as a Palouse farm center gathered momentum after 1892 when the University of Idaho opened there

Lewiston State Normal School's handsome Romanesque revival buildings were the pride of the community when completed at the turn of the century. A disastrous fire on December 5, 1917, gutted the structures. Only the portion at right was partially rebuilt and is still standing. Courtesy, Lewis-Clark State College

with six students and two professors. Including nearby farmers, Moscow had a population of more than 2,800 by 1890, and when university expansion supported an impressive business district, Moscow gradually surpassed eastern Washington Palouse towns to gain commercial supremacy over a wealthy farming area. Lewiston countered with a state college for teachers that opened in 1894. Although that institution could not match Moscow's university in potential for growth, Lewiston's river port helped compensate for Moscow's advantage as a rail center. Even by 1890, Lewiston's hotels and businesses were more substantial than its modest town population of 849 had indicated. By 1910 Lewiston grew to 6,043 compared with Moscow's 3,670. Lower Columbia navigation improvements helped Lewiston's river trade in 1914, and Moscow never began to catch up with Lewiston after that.

Farther north a promising new town of Coeur d'Alene had grown up adjacent to Fort Sherman, established in 1878 on a lakeshore site chosen by General William Tecumseh Sherman. Coeur d'Alene was in no position to overtake Spokane, which rose after 1890 to dominate a large area of Washington and Idaho, along with adjacent parts of Montana and British Columbia. But with an electric interurban streetcar line to Spokane, Coeur d'Alene gained an important advantage as Spokane's lakeshore resort.

Steamboat excursions from Coeur d'Alene became popular weekend recreational attractions. Coeur d'Alene became part of a larger urban complex, and after Heyburn State Park was

Facing page: Fort Sherman, named for Civil War General William Tecumseh Sherman, is now the site of North Idaho College in Coeur d'Alene. A replica of the gate shown in this photo of about 1890 can still be seen on the campus. The ornate stick-style building in the background is the post hospital. General Sherman himself paid a visit to the post in 1883 via the new Northern Pacific Railway. (ISHS)

The entire University of Idaho was housed in this picturesque Victorian Gothic building in Moscow in the 1890s. When fire destroyed it on March 30, 1906, the school had to virtually start over again. The new administration building was also Gothic, but of a type called "Collegiate Gothic." (ISHS)

Above: *Lost River Valley ranch children posed in front of their log cabin school in 1902. Many of them got to school on horseback. Teacher Ella Woods taught all eight grades. (ISHS)*

Left: *The one-room school was common on the Idaho frontier, but these children on the Boise Project, in sagebrush lands just being irrigated, attended school in a tent while a more permanent structure was being built. This was pioneer education at its most picturesque. (ISHS)*

Left, below: *Many of the new schoolhouses built in southwestern Idaho after the turn of the century were architecturally distinguished. Linder School, in Ada County west of Eagle, was an elegant example, but there were still less-than-elegant privies out back. The teacher in 1909 was Mary L. Evert. (ISHS)*

Above: *The entire student body of Albion State Normal School posed for this 1922 photograph. When the school was closed in 1951 several hundred of its graduates were teaching in Idaho public schools. The once-beautiful campus has been empty for most of the years since its abandonment. (ISHS)*

Right: *When Albion State Normal School received its first students in 1894, the entire operation was housed in this modest lava-rock building. Nothing else but barren sagebrush hills made up what would in time become an attractive campus with green lawns, shade trees, and several brick buildings. (ISHS)*

LAND RUSH

Pocatello's 1902 land rush attracted national attention. Ray Stannard Baker, already well-known as a journalist, came out to record it in a long article for *Century Magazine*. He did not try to get a ranch but joined an eager throng of aspiring claimants:

We have come down through the dust from Pocatello, past the lumber-yards, past the brewery, the top of which is already swarming with spectators, even beyond the cemetery; and we have brought with us every one in town and all the vehicles. They climb the Red Butte on our left, killing rattlesnakes as they go, and up the distant Brown Butte on our right. Here we are, cheerful, much excited, with the gray desert before us waiting the rush of our feet and the tramp of our horses. Some of us have taken off our shoes and sit our horses bare-back, that we may go light; others are in buggies, others on bicycles. . . .

They are off, neck and heel, driving home their spurs, doubled over their saddles, leaping sage-brush all confusion—riders, buggies, bicycles. At first, as we saw it from the end, the line held straight, with monstrous clouds of dust rising behind—a great cavalry charge. Then here and there riders sprang forward from the moving line, the distinction of the strong and the swift. But we are thrilled in vain. Up rises the dust, filling all the valley from Red Butte to Brown until nothing is left but a glimpse here and there of the moving gray phantom of a straggler. Behind, hopelessly and yet with boundless hope, trail two reeling white-topped wagons, their drivers leaning out in front, lashing their horses into dusty obscurity. And the last of the

The excitement of a land rush is vividly captured in this photo of would-be ranchers galloping onto the Fort Hall Indian Reservation on June 18, 1902, when portions of it were opened to settlement. The men at right are already staking their claim. Courtesy, Clifford Peake

honest runners has gone.

By mid-afternoon, a special Union Pacific train came by to pick up land claimants and take them north to Blackfoot where they could file their entries. There another stampede started as passengers began to jump out of coach windows to bypass crowded doorways as the train slowed down near their destination:

Who shall describe the unloading, the humorous haste and yet the grim seriousness of it? Men flying through the air, coat-tails spread, from cartop and window, rolling dustily from brake-beam and bumper, struggling from the vestibules, plunging down the steps, scattering across the sandy street, all noise and confusion. Some land on their heads on the platform, and go first

to the doctor; but most of the throng add themselves swiftly to the line which now reaches, closepacked, sinuous, from the doorway of the land office down the street. . . .

Within the land office everything is cool and orderly: a large room of white-plastered barrenness, a deal desk in front, a row of sober law-books, maps on the wall, a long, high stovepipe, a safe in the corner; clerks good-humored and busy; gigantic deputy in a helmet holding back the crowd at the door.

In one wild afternoon, Pocatello gained a host of new ranchers, and another disorderly land rush came to an end. After that a system for drawing land allotments by chance was generally employed to avoid repetition of Pocatello's "bustle and confusion" in distributing farmland.

The opening of new lands in Idaho's arid country created great excitement in the first decade of this century. Crowds gathered at Arco in 1909 to register for drawings on land in the Lost River Valley. (ISHS)

Pocatello was a lively railroad town when this picture was taken in a local saloon. There were a dozen such watering holes within a few blocks of the tracks. (ISHS)

established in 1909 as an upper Lake Coeur d'Alene resort, recreational opportunities were further enhanced. From a static population of about 500 in 1890 and 1900, Coeur d'Alene rose to 7,291 by 1910. North Idaho had one other lumber and resort city, Sandpoint, with about 3,000 people in 1910, and a mining center, Wallace, of equal size.

Farther south, Nampa and Caldwell competed for industry and trade in Boise Valley's growing irrigated area. Caldwell had started in 1883 as a railroad shipping and commercial center that would prosper as soon as irrigated farming could be developed there. A branch railroad to Boise was planned, but a national financial panic in 1884 halted canal and rail construction and delayed Caldwell's growth. Then in 1886 a rival Boise railroad connection was arranged at Nampa, nine miles away. By 1900 Nampa reached Caldwell's 1890 population level, while Caldwell had grown only to about 1,000. Each town still had excellent prospects. Caldwell's College of Idaho, which also served as a cultural center, opened in 1891 when Idaho had no other institu-

Right: *Typical of hundreds of fire lookout towers throughout Idaho's mountains is that on Bertha Hill, ten miles north of Headquarters, Idaho. (ISHS)*

Below: *This primitive logging operation beside the Clearwater used the muscle power of horses and men to get logs into the river for the drive downstream to the mill. The last Clearwater River drive took place in May 1971. Construction of Dworshak Dam and the filling of the reservoir ended this historic tradition. (ISHS)*

Right: *Steam locomotives had just about replaced horses and oxen in Idaho logging operations by 1910 when this picture was taken. A Shay locomotive, popularly known as a "sidewinder" because of its unusual gearing system, hauls logs out of a North Idaho forest. Courtesy, Museum of North Idaho*

Below: *The Barber Lumber Company of Wisconsin completed its big mill east of Boise in 1906. A dam and power plant were important parts of the operation, harnessing the energy of Boise River. The company town of Barber was erected nearby, and eventually a logging railroad was built up the river. (ISHS)*

FIRESTORM

Idaho's 1910 fire endangered many forest crews and threatened camps and communities over a wide area. Of those who escaped none had a more frightful time than Edward Pulaski's group trying to cross a high ridge to reach Wallace. A miner and plumber before he became a Forest Service ranger in 1908, Pulaski was a courageous field commander reminiscent of his great-grandfather, General Casimar Pulaski of George Washington's revolutionary army. One of Pulaski's fire fighters, an old Texas ranger and Indian fighter, described their ordeal:

One can not imagine what a roar of wind there was in those small canyons. The mountainsides everywhere were aflame and trees were falling in all directions all about us faster than one could count. The noise of the falling trees only added to the other din. It was terrible. In this frightful confusion we tore along in single file with Pulaski at the head. At times it would seem that the canyon in front of us was blocked with flame. Then Pulaski would order us to halt. He would take a gunnysack, soak it with water, place it over his head, dash through the smoke down the trail to see if the coast was clear. After assuring himself that everything was safe he would return to us and order us ahead. At last we reached the small tunnel and conditions were so bad then that he ordered us in. There was not sufficient room so Pulaski went ahead to a point where he knew there was a larger tunnel, telling us to remain behind, while he looked over the ground. He was absent but a few minutes when he returned and commanded us to follow him again. It was then that we got into the ill-fated tunnel, where six of the boys lost their lives. During all this terrible trip down the canyon Pulaski was just as cool as he could be. He kept telling them that they would get out safely, but that it was necessary to hold together. He stayed outside the tunnel till all got in and then took his station at the mouth to keep the timbers from getting on fire and pre-vent the flames from entering. It was while fighting the flames at the mouth of the tunnel that he sustained the injury to one of his eyes that was thought might result in blindness.

Several hours later, Pulaski's crew began to revive and to stumble and crawl down a rocky two-mile trail through burning timber to Wallace. Pulaski was temporarily blind and in terrible shape, but he recovered. He continued as a forest ranger for twenty more years. Among other achievements, he helped develop a special fire-fighting tool that combined an axe and a pick on a single handle—a useful piece of equipment named a "pulaski" in his honor. Pulaski's escape route and mine tunnel are listed in the National Register of Historic Places.

Ranger Edward Pulaski, hero of the 1910 North Idaho fire, saved most of his crew of fire-fighters through cool courage and resourcefulness. He is shown here near the mine tunnel which sheltered his men during one of the worst forest fires in U.S. history. A standard forest tool widely used today is called a "pulaski" after him. Courtesy, U.S. Forest Service

Roads were built to provide access to timbered areas, for fire protection as well as logging and recreation. National forests were managed for conservation objectives, with improved defense against fire a primary goal. Cooperative fire protection agencies, which had organized earlier, were expanded after 1911 when federal legislation provided matching funds to states with forest protection agencies. State and private timberland owners funded regional systems of lookouts and fire crews to guard non-federal lands. Idaho had four associations and eighteen national forests, each offering fire protection to endangered timber.

In addition to fire protection, Idaho's loggers had to invest heavily in transportation systems. Log drives had been used in several southwestern Idaho rivers for more than forty years to supply local sawmills. Boise and Payette river log drives were dangerous for loggers, who came primarily from Maine, where stream conditions were different from those in Idaho. Accidents occurred frequently. In explaining a fatality in 1901, a press account noted "It is very common for loggers to fall into the water. Usually no attention is paid to them in such a case." When commercial lumber companies started large log drives, their casualty rate reached unacceptable levels. Ten loggers were lost in 1907. As a consequence, expensive railroad construction was necessary to get logs to sawmills built after 1912. North Idaho also needed logging railroads for some areas, although horses and oxen continued to haul logs to landings where river transportation was available.

Unanticipated competition from forest-products industries in several southern states presented another challenge to Idaho logging, restricting Idaho's sales area to northern midwestern markets. Unlike Great Lakes and Pacific Northwest forests, southern timber grew too quickly to be chopped out entirely, even by heavy logging. Despite southern competition, however, Idaho's lumbering industry continued to expand, exceeding mining in economic importance. Only seven states could match Idaho in acres of forestland, and two decades of commercial logging after 1900 did not make too great a dent in forest resources. Construction of a large, modern mill in Lewiston in 1926 brought even further expansion to Idaho's lumber industry.

Idaho's loggers, like all lumbermen, shared a forest lore that spread from one camp to another as transient timber cutters moved about their mountain domain. Tall tales were a specialty everywhere. Jim Stevens, who got his start in Idaho sawmill

Jim Stevens, who attended Weiser's Intermountain Institute as a teenager, attained fame as the author of stories about Paul Bunyan, a lumberjack legend with a great blue ox named Babe. Stevens used loggers' tall tales as the basis for his books. (ISHS)

Loggers had hearty appetites. This lumber camp dining hall crew awaits the onslaught of a thundering herd of hungry men. Since most utensils in this kitchen and dining room were metal, there was little breakage, no matter how rough the crew, but the noise must have been deafening. (ISHS)

camps, began to publish articles and books on Paul Bunyan in 1925. These gained widespread popularity, and other writers joined in making Paul Bunyan and other loggers' legends into a national tradition.

By that time lumbering in Idaho had achieved a solid development with a long-range future, largely because southern competition as well as the inherent hazards and difficulties of early logging methods had defeated ambitious attempts to chop down all commercial timber in a decade or two. Even Paul Bunyan and his blue ox could not clear timber off Idaho's mountain ridges in as thorough and systematic a manner as Michigan, Wisconsin, and Minnesota had been harvested. Eventually conservation practices and planning for reforestation, under which timber became a renewable crop, gave Idaho's forest-product industries a permanent future.

VI
The Desert Blooms, Farms Flourish

Idaho's greatest rate of sustained permanent expansion came shortly after 1900. Huge new irrigated tracts came under cultivation, and large canals expanded some earlier farming areas. By 1909 all of Idaho's major population centers had been established. Early in the twentieth century small towns served the needs of local farmers. But the automobile soon changed everything. Suburban development replaced nineteenth-century villages, and farming areas came to depend upon central cities. Small independent communities went into a slow decline after 1920.

Agricultural technology, capable of processing new crops, also encouraged important changes after 1900. Sugar factories brought a major new farming specialty to Idaho. Late in 1890 construction began on a pioneer beet sugar plant in Lehi, Utah, and within a decade Mormon sugar developers were preparing to expand their enterprise into Idaho. After 1900 their increased production attracted national attention, and Mormon beet sugar production was incorporated into an expanded nationwide sugar trust. This provided capital for development of Idaho plants near Idaho Falls in 1903 and between Rexburg and Saint Anthony in 1904. A plant built in Nampa in 1906 introduced sugar beets to southwestern Idaho, and other factories followed. Problems with crop disease in 1905 and with loss of tariff protection in 1913 restricted Idaho's early sugar production, but after 1914 the European war provided large new markets. International sugar shortages stimulated production, and Idaho Falls became a major center for beet seed crops when French and German sources were cut off. With rapid expansion of irrigated farming in Idaho after 1900, particularly around Twin Falls and Burley, sugar beet processing contributed a new cash crop to a growing agricultural economy.

Idaho entrepreneur I.B. Perrine gave the agricultural economy

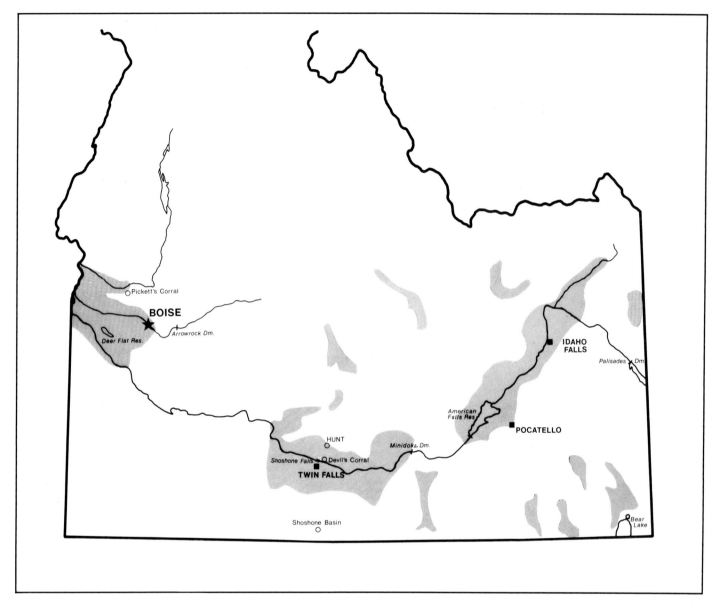

another boost. At his Blue Lakes ranch below Shoshone Falls in 1884, he learned how irrigation could produce marvelous crops of hay and grain. With profits from stockraising and gold mining on his ranch, he planted an orchard and berry bushes as well. With a stage stop and a hotel, Perrine had a diversified farm and tourist enterprise that demonstrated what could be done in a vast desert expanse.

After sixteen years of ranching, he decided to go ahead with a major irrigation project. Filing for enough water to operate a sixty-five-mile canal, Perrine commenced his bold undertaking in 1900. No gravity system so ambitious had been developed since Babylonian times, but Perrine got Stanley B. Milner, a Salt Lake capitalist, to fund his ditch surveys and Frank H. Buhl, a Pittsburgh investor in western mines, to advance $1,500,000 for

Facing page: *Early twentieth century reclamation projects, indicated by gray areas, significantly expanded Idaho's agricultural resources and created new cities and a booming economy. Courtesy, Don Watts*

Right top: *I.B. Perrine's great Blue Lakes Ranch was a marvel of pioneering enterprise in the midst of an awesome and desolate lava rock canyon. Perrine located here in the 1880s and raised fruit that won gold medals at Paris in 1900, Buffalo in 1901, St. Louis in 1904, and Seattle in 1909. He also promoted the development of Twin Falls. Courtesy, State Historical Society of Wisconsin*

Right, bottom: *Sugar City, Idaho, took its name from the local industry that gave it birth. These sugar beet farmers are unloading their wagons outside the big brick refining plant about 1910. Today's beets, delivered by truck and moved by conveyor belts, are twice as large as these early ones. (ISHS)*

construction. A townsite for Twin Falls was established in 1904, in the center of the proposed project, and within two years a modern city had been built there.

Perrine followed with a matching canal system north of Twin Falls, serving Jerome and other new communities there. His success in advertising and promoting such a mammoth reclamation venture created an agricultural empire of 385,000 acres in a previously uninhabited desert.

Perrine's dramatic success encouraged a substantial number of similar ventures in south-central Idaho. Most of them ran into serious problems, and several proved to be total failures. Some did not have enough water available, even in wet years. Others had engineering and management problems. Most were short of capital needed to start up a large irrigation development.

In order to obtain the necessary capital and engineering de-

The Union Pacific crosses Snake River at American Falls. When this 1910 view was taken a long steel bridge had replaced the earlier wooden one and the power plant, center, was generating electricity for the nearby town of American Falls. In 1927 a dam built above the falls created American Falls reservoir, and the town was moved to higher ground. (ISHS)

barriers, and a long-desired route from Lewiston to Missoula was projected. Southern Idaho communities also received road connections that served farmers as well as miners and loggers.

After 1914 wartime disruptions in Europe affected Idaho's farmers in ways that had not been foreseen. Twentieth-century industrialized warfare devastated and disorganized large parts of Europe. Rising crop prices and greater demand for U.S. crops soon resulted.

Idaho's farmers responded to international demand with increased production. They also began to organize to protect themselves economically. Regional and national farmers' unions, such as North Dakota's Nonpartisan League, followed earlier National Grange efforts to give Idaho farmers political clout.

Idaho did not have the industrial capacity to produce munitions or build ships, but Idaho's farmers were expected to make a major contribution to essential wartime food production. Shortages of wheat and meat became a national problem. Even after Germany was defeated late in 1918, farm products were needed on a major scale. In 1919 agricultural prices reached a peak. After that, a revival of European production brought a difficult new era for Idaho farmers. Possibilities for apparently limitless expansion of Idaho's crops came to an abrupt halt. Two decades of unparalleled growth gave way to an era of adjustment to hard times.

Above: *When Governor Moses Alexander signed Prohibition into law on March 1, 1915, the large crowd present included representatives of the Anti-Saloon League, the WCTU, the legislature, and the clergy. (ISHS)*

Right: *The people of Challis celebrated the end of World War I by burning the Kaiser in effigy on November 11, 1918 — Armistice Day. (ISHS)*

VII
Lean Years and War Years

By 1920 Idaho had benefited from two decades of expansion in both agriculture and lumbering. Major lode mines had continued to pour out mineral wealth, and transportation improvements were about to encourage a lively tourist economy. Population had increased dramatically, so local markets accounted for a growing share of Idaho's farm and forest products. A wave of prosperity encouraged farmers to enlarge their holdings at high prices and helped investors develop new businesses. Then abrupt national economic collapse brought wartime and postwar farm prosperity to a sudden halt in 1920. Two decades of disaster and depression followed.

In common with other western farm states, Idaho did not prosper for two decades after 1920. This kind of slow-down had not been anticipated, and bankers and industrial managers were as unprepared as farmers and loggers to decide what to do when they faced a series of financial crises that halted population growth for a decade.

Farmers were injured more than industrial producers and professional groups when prices declined after May 1920. Within a year farm products were worth only 63 percent of what they had been in comparison with industrial commodity prices. An unprecedented epidemic of bank failures resulted from Idaho's agricultural depression. Bank investment in suddenly worthless farm mortgages spread economic ruin to other Idaho industries. Congress, with assistance from a variety of national farm organizations, tried without success to find an acceptable solution to very difficult problems in agricultural economics. More than a decade of unfavorable farm commodity prices and crop surpluses inflicted severe penalties upon rural states like Idaho.

In spite of adversity, Idaho's reclamation projects, notably Twin Falls and Minidoka, continued to expand with long-term federal loans. American Falls Reservoir, completed in 1927,

Facing page: *Oneida County dry farms, like this one photographed by Arthur Rothstein in 1936, were marginal in the best of times. The Great Depression forced owners and tenants alike to move out or starve. Thousands of such one-family farms and ranches are now consolidated in large corporate operations. Courtesy,* The American West in the Thirties, *Dover Publications*

VIII
Industrialists and Environmentalists

Diversification of Idaho's industrial production accounted for many notable changes in the state's development after 1946. Products such as mobile homes and recreational vehicles appropriate for regional markets or suitable for easy transport were added to Idaho's manufacturing potential. A state with a small, scattered population remote from heavy industry and much raw material had to be selective in choosing products for manufacturing. An abundance of inexpensive hydroelectric power compensated in part for lack of oil and coal, but most kinds of heavy industry were excluded from Idaho's economy.

Phosphate mining in southeastern Idaho grew from modest beginnings in 1906 into a major postwar enterprise. Wartime production of superphosphate for fertilizers, essential for increased farm crops, had begun in Pocatello in 1944. In 1948 the plant was greatly enlarged to provide expanded production of an improved ammonia superphosphate, utilizing ore from above Fort Hall. Within a decade about one million tons of rock were processed annually. An elemental-phosphorous electric furnace followed in 1949, accounting for another 600,000 tons of ore per year within a decade. An additional large elemental phosphorous furnace complex was constructed at Soda Springs in 1952. Along with earlier established producers, these plants transformed southeastern Idaho's industrial economy and supported an agricultural revolution as well by providing fertilizer for crops.

Northwest of Pocatello, an entirely different transformation took place. In 1949 Atomic Energy Commission officials brought a giant new industry to southeastern Idaho's naval gun-testing range. Located in a desert remote from large population centers but favored by a large underground water supply, Idaho's National Reactor Testing Station offered an attractive location for nuclear-engineering plants in an area where earthquakes were unknown. Within two years a practical nuclear-powered electri-

Facing Page: *F-111A fighter bombers from Mountain Home Air Force Base fly regularly over Idaho's mountains and deserts. This one was photographed over Redfish Lake in the Sawtooth range. Courtesy, United States Air Force*

cal generating system was completed. Work began on nuclear submarine engines and other devices scarcely imagined a decade earlier. As headquarters of this operation, Idaho Falls grew rapidly. A large number of engineers and nuclear-research specialists introduced a significant new element into Idaho's population.

Military installations continued as an important element in Idaho's economy after 1946. Mountain Home Air Force Base reopened for a time in 1948 as a training facility for a Strategic Air Command photographic unit, after which it served as a Military Air Transport Service base for almost one year. In 1953 Strategic Air Command bombers and refueling planes were stationed there. A decade later three Titan missile sites were added to Mountain Home's military complex for two years. In 1966 Tactical Air Command reconnaissance planes replaced bombers and missiles at Mountain Home. An electronic combat squadron in 1981 brought in a new weapons system to detect and render ineffective any hostile missile system. With Idaho's greatest concentration of capital and a staff of several thousand, Mountain Home Air Force Base continues to have an impact upon local industrial development.

Recreational-vehicle and mobile-home fabrication proved to be practical additions to southwestern Idaho's industrial development. A mobile-home plant established in Boise in 1954 developed business sufficient to encourage the opening of similar plants in Nampa, Caldwell, and Weiser. By 1967 Idaho's eleven mobile-home plants were doing an annual business of more than $27,000,000. Less than a decade later, the value of their yearly product exceeded $100,000,000. Recreational vehicles—mostly camping units—augmented Idaho's housing fabrication industry, which commanded a wide western market.

Expansion of food-processing, particularly from Jack Simplot's large wartime potato- and onion-dehydrating plants, accounted for a still more significant industrial diversification. Simplot transferred his attention to frozen foods that were more acceptable commercially and to potato-processing for fast-food outlets that became popular after1946. Other large companies followed his lead, and major plants at Burley, Caldwell, and Idaho Falls processed about two-thirds of Idaho's potato production by 1974. Enlarged sugar factories in Nampa, Paul, Twin Falls, and Idaho Falls gave added impetus to beet-raising. Meat-processing plants near Boise were eventually enlarged into major industrial enter-

By the "Roaring Twenties" the University of Idaho had an impressive campus. Many students drove automobiles, and parking them had already become a problem for the school administration. Notice that most of the cars in this 1922 photo are parked on the lawn. The 1908 Administration Building at left replaces the one destroyed by fire in 1906. Courtesy, University of Idaho

prises, and egg and poultry production turned into giant assembly-line operations at Franklin and Meridian.

Farming also assumed a new industrial form. Agricultural equipment had undergone one series of improvements after another for more than a century before 1946. Wartime labor shortages had helped create a system under which fewer farmers produced larger crops. Postwar mechanization continued this trend on a rapidly increasing scale. Migrant workers were brought in from Texas, California, and Arizona to thin beets, harvest crops that could not be handled mechanically, and take on other laborious tasks that no one else wanted to do.

As fast as possible new equipment was employed to supplant hand labor of any kind. Irrigation ditches gradually were replaced by pipe and sprinkler systems. Advanced computer systems were employed to determine crop yields and values, cost-account individual farm operations, determine what crops to produce, and to control planting, watering, and harvesting activities. Even family farms were incorporated as business enterprises, and large, consolidated farming companies gained increasingly greater importance. University research programs made many of these changes possible, and farm equipment manufacturers contributed to agricultural innovation. Production controls and marketing systems continued to be a problem, but farmers operated at less of a disadvantage than they had between 1920 and 1940.

Universities and colleges—essential for modern industrial development as well as for improved farming and stockraising methods—experienced sudden growth in 1946 when thousands of returning veterans resumed their interrupted education. New institutions had to be developed to meet greatly increased demands for higher education; existing facilities had to be enlarged. North Idaho had a state university in Moscow, a state teachers' college in Lewiston, and a district junior college in Coeur d'Alene as a base for expansion in 1946. Conversion of Farragut Naval Training Station into yet another college helped to relieve enrollment pressures for several years, before this institution became a state park.

Independent private colleges in Caldwell, Nampa, and Rexburg provided educational opportunities in southern Idaho for those who did not go to a teachers' college in Albion, a district junior college in Boise, or a state university branch campus in Pocatello. Graduate programs were available at the University of

Idaho, and only two others—the College of Idaho and Northwest Nazarene College—were regular degree-granting institutions. Professional degrees in elementary education were available at Lewiston and Albion and in pharmacy at Pocatello, but only a few students completed these curricula. This situation changed rather quickly.

Elementary and secondary education were also strengthened by school district consolidation, accomplished after several years of effort to achieve economy as well as to offer better programs in larger high schools. Opportunities for vocational education and vocational rehabilitation were also improved. Coordination of instruction at all levels had been mandated by a constitutional amendment in 1912 that provided for central overall management of public education under a single state board of education. After 1946 professional staffs were employed to help local school boards and university administrators meet a variety of needs in an expanding industrial society.

University and other educational professionals supported cultural activities in Idaho communities as both the population and interest grew in art and literature. Dramatic and musical performances, traditional in Idaho's frontier communities, gained an added impetus in college communities that provided professional sources of performing talent.

Idaho already had nationally prominent novelists as well as lo-

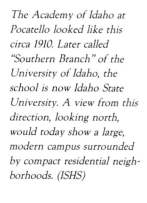

The Academy of Idaho at Pocatello looked like this circa 1910. Later called "Southern Branch" of the University of Idaho, the school is now Idaho State University. A view from this direction, looking north, would today show a large, modern campus surrounded by compact residential neighborhoods. (ISHS)

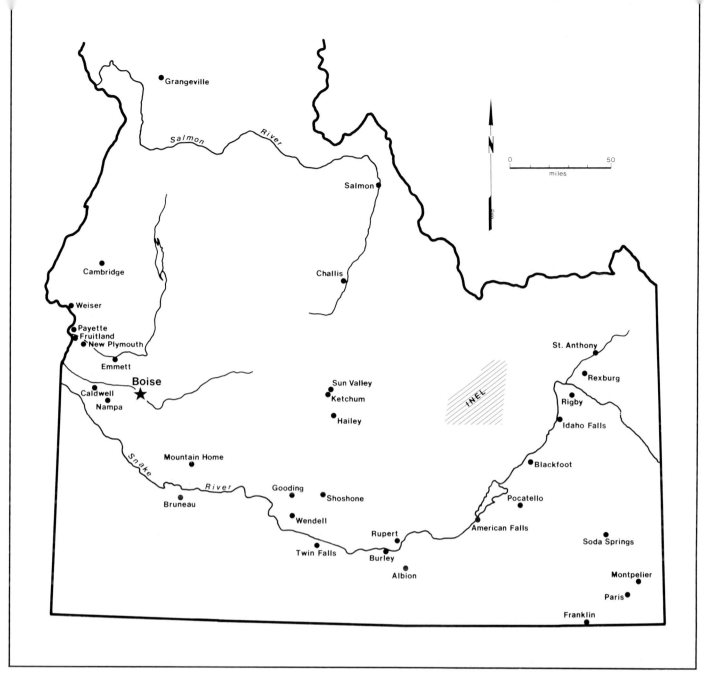

Grangeville

Salmon River

Salmon

Challis

Cambridge

Weiser

Payette
Fruitland
New Plymouth

Emmett

Boise

Caldwell
Nampa

St. Anthony

Rexburg

Sun Valley
Ketchum

Hailey

INEL

Rigby

Idaho Falls

Mountain Home

Snake River

Gooding

Shoshone

Bruneau

Wendell

Rupert

Twin Falls

Burley

Albion

American Falls

Blackfoot

Pocatello

Soda Springs

Montpelier

Paris

Franklin

0   50
miles

N

Above: *The Idaho National Engineering Laboratory brought the nuclear energy industry to south Idaho. Idaho Falls grew rapidly as a result. Courtesy, Don Watts*

cally significant authors and teachers. Vardis Fisher, who grew up in an isolated upper Snake River Mormon community, had achieved national distinction for his series of psychological novels and for his portrayal of western themes. Expanding upon his earlier contributions, Fisher undertook an ambitious sequence of a dozen novels designed to interpret human morality. Turning to western history, he dealt with explorers, mountain men, gold camps, and Mormons, in novels and non-fiction works.

Idaho's spectacular outdoor environment attracted Ernest Hemingway to settle in Ketchum after 1958. Hemingway had spent three autumn seasons hunting and writing at Sun Valley from 1939 to 1941. During that time he worked on and published his novel *For Whom the Bell Tolls*. After a wartime interruption, he returned each fall between 1946 and 1948 before settling in Ketchum a decade later.

Expanding opportunities for recreational development also affected all parts of Idaho after 1946. Wildlife management areas were set aside to provide sanctuaries for fish and game, which needed more than simple legal protection from excessive exploitation. A professionally staffed state fish and game department undertook management surveys to determine wildlife populations and needs. In addition a research program to improve stream and game habitats and investigate wildlife problems led to new policies that offered more adequate environmental protection. Population growth and tourism made such professional fish and game management more necessary than ever before. Maintenance of good hunting and fishing resources, in turn, helped to attract more population and industry. Tourism also increased as a result of Idaho's success with fish hatcheries and wildlife development programs. Although lower Snake and Columbia power dams created obstacles that threatened and diminished major salmon and steelhead runs, by 1984 Idaho was beginning to have a voice in regional management of those resources as well.

Competing interests for use of Idaho's abundant water supply brought on several major conflicts over river development after 1948. Power producers needed hydroelectric dams with reasonably steady stream flows. Irrigated lands required large storage reservoirs that diverted almost all summer river flows. Salmon and steelhead fisheries could not tolerate dams for either power or irrigation on streams used by migrating fish. Flood control dams also destroyed fish runs and were not entirely compatible

Above: *Crooner Bing Crosby was a frequent visitor to Idaho throughout his life, especially to hunt, fish, and play golf. In 1950 he came to Boise to campaign for his old friend Herman Welker in his successful bid for the U.S. Senate. Crosby and Welker had been golfing buddies in Southern California years before. Courtesy, Mrs. Herman Welker*

Facing page: *Writer Ernest Hemingway, at age sixty, kicked a beer can along a Sun Valley road. He settled in Ketchum in 1958 and lived there until his death in 1961. Courtesy, John Bryson*

Above: *Lake Pend d'Oreille,
Idaho's largest, is a favorite
destination for vacationers.
Courtesy, Andrew Rafkind*

The Palouse is one of the great wheat-producing areas of the West. In autumn its rolling hills under dazzling skies and drifting clouds create a panorama of constantly changing beauty. The clouds bring enough rain to grow grain without irrigation. Courtesy, Arthur A. Hart

Top: *Margaretta Brown was
one of Idaho's earliest artists.
She was at her best when
painting scenes like this of
hydraulic mining near Idaho
City. In meticulous detail she
shows men with hydraulic
nozzles, called "giants," wash-
ing away a high gravel bank.
The material was then run
through cleated sluice boxes
to extract the gold dust it
contained. (ISHS)*

Above: *George W. Russell's
ranch east of Boise City, established in 1864, looked like
this in the 1880s. The house,
built in 1868, is still standing.
The Russell property became
the site of dozens of the
city's finest mansions after
Warm Springs Avenue be-
came fashionable in the
1890s. (ISHS)*

157

Above: *Mount Idaho, one of North Idaho's oldest towns, lost its importance after Grangeville was founded a few miles away on Camas Prairie. Apple blossoms brighten a wet spring day on the quiet old town's wooded mountainside. Courtesy, Arthur A. Hart.*

Sacred Heart Mission, near Cataldo, is Idaho's oldest building. Jesuit Father Antonio Ravalli, drawing upon his Italian background, designed a truly remarkable church, combining baroque and classical elements. He supervised lay brothers and Coeur d'Alene Indians in its construction. Ravalli himself crafted much of the furniture and interior ornamentation. Courtesy, Ernest J. Lombard

Tim Goodale brought Oregon Trail pioneers over Cat Creek summit into the drainage of Boise River's south fork beginning in 1862. This is an April 1976 view from Highway 68 looking west, about seventy-five miles from Boise. Courtesy, Arthur A. Hart

Running the rapids is a popular thrill on the Payette River at Banks, Idaho, site of annual whitewater competition. Courtesy, Andrew Rafkind

Visitors enjoy Idaho's beauty from horseback near Crouch. Courtesy, Andrew Rafkind

172

Above: *City-dwellers of Boise do not have to give up the clean air and open spaces of the country. Boiseans enjoy strolls and softball in Ann Morrison Park. Courtesy, Andrew Rafkind*

Facing page: *Fireworks and the lights of Boise below create a dramatic Fourth of July tableau. Courtesy, Andrew Rafkind*

The United First Financial Center is a strikingly modern building in Boise. Courtesy, Andrew Rafkind

Above: *Dawn breaks at Harriman State Park, and the early morning mist lends an eerie beauty to the sunrise. Courtesy, Andrew Rafkind*

Facing page: *Idaho has more acres of wilderness than any state except Alaska, and Idahoans know how to preserve and enjoy their great outdoors. This Idahoan has pitched her tent at Sage Hen Reservoir. Courtesy, Andrew Rafkind*

Below: *Ballooning is a popular sport in Idaho, and these colorful participants compete in the annual "hound and hare" competition in Boise. Courtesy, Andrew Rafkind*

SYMMS FRUIT RANCH

The family-owned Symms Fruit Ranch dominates Sunny Slope south of Caldwell, an area of rich soil and splendid fruit trees. What started as an eighty-acre homestead in 1913 has become a 2,700-acre operation.

Apples are the mainstay of the ranch, which produced 800,000 bushels annually in the mid-1980s. It also produces peaches, cherries, plums, pears, and grapes. Some of the acres grow row crops, such as onions and potatoes. Cattle also are raised.

Grapes comprise the newest crop in the fruit line, and the end result is Idaho's largest winery, which is also the second-largest winery in the Pacific Northwest. Ste. Chapelle, which took form in 1976, has attained an international reputation. The Symms family owns 80 percent of the winery, which was founded in 1976. Ste. Chapelle is housed on the side of a hill amid rows of grapes in a building designed to look like the church of Ste. Chapelle in Paris.

R.A. Symms arrived at Sunny Slope with his wife and three children in 1913 and was able to purchase an eighty-acre homestead. The next year he planted eight acres of orchard, which included varieties of apples, cherries, peaches, plums, and pears.

As Symms gradually enlarged his

Ste. Chapelle, Idaho's largest winery, is the second largest in the Northwest.

holdings, his two sons, Darwin and Doyle, labored with him in the struggle to clear sagebrush, deter jack rabbits, and grow and market their fruit.

Darwin, born in 1899, became a partner with his father upon his graduation from college in 1928 and the business was named Symms Fruit Ranch at that time. He also married Irene Knowlton that year. Doyle was born in 1909 and became a partner upon his graduation from college in 1931, the year he married Myrtle Smith. All the while the business was

Symms Fruit Ranch in Idaho's Sunny Slope.

buying more land and planting more orchards.

In 1928 the family built a packing shed to package and sell their own fruit. As the Great Depression struck the price of fruit fell to almost unbelievable lows. But the family prevailed and even planted more acres of orchards. R.A. Symms died in 1934; his wife, Eva, died in 1945.

Times improved and the brothers acquired more land and planted more fruit trees. Packinghouses were built to package the growing volume of fruit. The latest in automated machinery was used. In the mid-1950s cold-storage plants were constructed. As the business grew, packing plants were enlarged and additional cold storages were added to handle the increasing volume of apples and other fruits. Modern controlled-atmosphere storages now permit prime quality apples to be shipped any month of the year.

Darwin and Irene have four children: Shirley Maggard, Virginia Kleweno, Dick, and Steve. Steve was elected to the U.S. House of Representatives in 1972. He has been a member of the U.S. Senate since 1980. Doyle and Myrtle had three children: Carolyn, who died in 1945; Kathy Mertz; and Bill.

Doyle died in 1983. Darwin is now chairman of the board, Dick is president of the corporation, and Jim Mertz, Doyle's son-in-law, is secretary. Dan Symms, Steve's son, has joined the firm as the first member of the fourth generation in the family business.

BOISE STATE UNIVERSITY

Economically, 1932, during the depth of the Great Depression, was the worst of times to begin a venture in higher education. But in September of that year Idaho Episcopal Bishop Middleton Barnwell opened Boise Junior College at St. Margaret's Hall, a girls' school the church had operated since 1892. There were seventy students and eight full-time faculty members.

By the mid-1980s that tiny junior college had become an institution with the largest head-count enrollment among the state's three universities. Its campus glittered with buildings of architectural efficiency dedicated to all undergraduate and a few graduate curricula of higher education. They included a large pavilion and a "talk-of-the-town" center for the performing arts.

This early 1940s photograph is of the campus of Boise Junior College.

By the end of the second year of operation, the church could no longer support the school, so Barnwell turned to the Boise Chamber of Commerce. Unwilling to lose the economic and cultural benefits of a college inside the city limits, the chamber provided some financial assistance and helped form a nonprofit corporation to govern the school. The chamber's commitment to Boise Junior College spurred countless community efforts that contributed to the growth of the school despite the depressed economy.

On June 7, 1934, Boise Junior College was officially incorporated with a seven-member board of trustees headed by attorney O.O. Haga. Two years later the trustees selected one of the first faculty members, Eugene B. Chaffee, to serve as the school's president. The college began to grow under his guidance and promotion. Chaffee and the board successfully

lobbied the legislature to allow the establishment of junior college taxing districts. In 1939 Boiseans voted to create the Boise Junior College District, putting the school on a more solid foundation of revenue from property and liquor taxes.

The growing school needed more room, so the trustees decided to relocate the campus across the Boise River on the site of the abandoned Boise Municipal Airport. Using a $57,000 Works Progress Administration grant, new topsoil was brought in to cover the gravel runways. In September 1940 the school moved into its new quarters. At the center of the otherwise vacant campus was the brand-new red brick administration building, which for years contained most classrooms, offices, and the library for the junior college. Students enjoyed their campus for less than a year before World War II began and shook the world. Students and faculty enlisted in the military. By 1942 enrollment had dropped to about 200. Only twenty-seven men enrolled in the spring of 1945, and a pilot training program on campus kept the school from closing.

The war ended just in time for fall classes in 1945. Encouraged by the GI Bill, students returned to campus in record numbers, and the junior college did its best to accommodate the renewed demands for higher education in Boise.

The campus skyline changed dramatically throughout the 1950s and 1960s as citizens of Boise supported bond issues to construct new buildings at the school. In 1956 its enrollment topped 1,000 for the first time. In its first three decades Boise Junior College served the educational needs of Treasure Valley and received the warm support of its residents.

By the early 1960s the demands had outstripped the resources of the junior college. It was time for a four-year college in Idaho's largest city; in 1964 Governor Robert E. Smylie signed landmark legislation that changed BJC's name to Boise College and allowed the school to offer bach-

elor's degrees. Enrollment jumped 40 percent, straining the school as it struggled to upgrade its faculty, curricula, library, and buildings.

In 1967, after thirty-one years at the helm of BJC, president Eugene Chaffee retired. His legacy was a school that was nationally known academically and athletically, yet one that remained community and student oriented. Dr. John Barnes, president of Arizona Western College in Yuma, was named to succeed. That same year Governor Don Samuelson signed legislation bringing Boise College into the state system of higher education as Boise State College. As of January 1, 1969, it became a state-supported school with statewide responsibilities.

Enrollments increased at a heavy pace during the 1970s. Under state support, new academic programs were added, more faculty were hired, and the campus family of buildings continued to grow. In 1974 Governor Cecil D. Andrus signed the bill changing the name of the institution to Boise State University. The university status gave the school a growing role in the state's educational system.

President John Barnes resigned in 1977 after leading the university through ten dynamic years. Most of the campus was built, many new academic programs were added, enrollment more than doubled, and the budget quadrupled under his tenure. The new president, Dr. John Keiser, came aboard in 1978 after serving as acting president at Sangamon State University in Springfield, Illinois.

In the 1980s Boise State University continued its tradition of growth and leadership in quality education. It forged a unique partnership with the Boise community to construct three buildings. The Pavilion (1982) and Morrison Center for the Performing Arts (1984) provide the university with unsurpassed facilities for events of all kinds. The Simplot/Micron Center for Technology (1985) brings state-of-the-art education delivery systems and technical programs to

The campus of Boise State University today.

the Treasure Valley. Because BSU is in the commercial and governmental center of Idaho, students find employment and internships that enhance classroom learning. As Idaho's urban university, BSU offers students a blend of cultural, recreational, social, and educational opportunities not found elsewhere in the state.

The university is the home of two recent Rhodes scholars, two Fulbright professors, a Truman scholar, and internationally known researchers, in fields as diverse as political science, geology, business, psychology, and mathematics.

Its traditions of academic excellence and community service, along with an enthusiastic faith in the future, make Boise State University one of the West's most dynamic institutions of higher learning.

SUNSHINE MINING COMPANY

The year 1984 was the 100th anniversary of the discovery of a silver-bearing lode on Big Creek, near Kellogg, and it led to the ultimate establishment of the Sunshine Mine, one of the world's top silver producers. In fact, since September 1884 the mine has yielded over 300 million ounces of silver, or more than the combined total of all the mines in the famous Comstock Lode in Nevada.

A significant event took place in the year of the 100th anniversary. Sunshine Mining Company moved its headquarters from Kellogg to Boise, the state's capital city. It was the first time a mining company of Sunshine's size was headquartered in Boise. There was reason for the move. Since Sunshine has mining properties in California, Nevada, and Utah, as well as northern Idaho, Boise was a logical center for its operations.

The mine was discovered by Dennis and True Blake as they scrambled up the east side of Big Creek Canyon and found an outcropping a few hundred feet below the top of the ridge. Samples proved to be high in silver. The

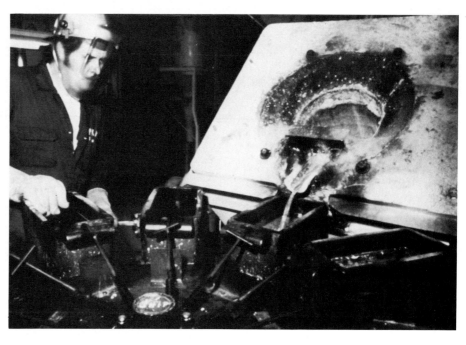

A refinery man pours molten silver into 1,000-ounce molds.

Blakes toiled by hand and with primitive tools for thirty years on their Yankee Boy claims. In due course Yankee Boy and other claims were taken over by the Sunshine Mining Company, which was incorporated in 1919.

But it was not until 1931 that the bonanza of high-grade ore was found, and Sunshine moved rapidly into the group of high silver producers. In 1937, when it yielded 12,147,719 ounces of silver, Sunshine became the largest producer of silver from any mine in the world.

Throughout its existence the company has undergone the vicissitudes of labor problems, price and supply-and-demand variations, and fires, but as a preeminent silver producer it never lost its economic vitality.

In the early 1950s it appeared that Sunshine might run out of its silver ore reserves. The company, told by geologists the mine could last no more than ten years, began buying up other properties nearby and began exploration on a large scale. Ultimately, rich veins were uncovered at deeper levels.

Sunshine used the best available technology and equipment as the years went by. In the early 1960s rock bolting was substituted for supporting timbers, long used underground. New equipment made it more efficient to drive drifts and crosscuts and to work in the stopes.

When the firm reached its 100th year, its shafts and workings extended to a depth of 6,000 feet, or 3,300 feet below sea level. The workings covered a lateral area three miles long and two miles wide. The width of the mineralized veins average two to five feet, but they have reached as

The surface facilities of Sunshine Mining Company, located on Big Creek near Kellogg in the famous Coeur d'Alene Mining District.

wide as thirty feet.

Access to the mine is gained through the Jewell Shaft, which extends downward to a depth of 4,000 feet. All ore, waste rock, supplies, and the miners are hoisted in this shaft. Two other shafts extend downward and provide access to the ore bodies. Sunshine has used what is called a cut-and-fill method of mining. Large blocks of rock, 200 feet long by 200 feet high, within which the ore body exists, are mined from the bottom toward the top in what are known as stopes. The miners produce the 1,000 tons of ore a day needed to keep the crusher and refineries in operation at the surface.

A by-product of the ore is antimony, used to harden lead and as a fireproofing agent for textiles. Sunshine is the largest domestic producer of the metal. A recently constructed silver refinery has a capacity of up to 50,000 ounces of silver and 1,200 ounces of gold each day. Also obtained in the refining process is up to 7,000 pounds of high-grade copper daily.

Sunshine's silver goes to customers around the world, mostly to industrial users such as photographic and electronic firms, makers of solar-energy devices, the medical profession, and to silverware and jewelry artisans. The company sells silver directly to investors and others in the form of bullion and medallions.

Sunshine has undergone two takeovers since the mid-1960s, but it never lost its identity. New York investors began an effort in 1961 to acquire the mine, and in 1965 new directors were substituted for the old and a new regime began. In a few years the firm began to diversify, expanding into electronics, metal fabrication, and other businesses not related to mining.

In 1977 Great Western United Corporation won sufficient stock proxies to assume control. Sunshine was at a low ebb. A year-long strike in 1976 came on the heels of a long rehabilitation of the mine following a disastrous fire in 1972 that took the

Early-day miners, in the Coeur d'Alene Mining District, used emerging technology and picks and shovels.

lives of ninety-one men.

Sunshine liquidated itself of all the unrelated businesses, and in an annual report said the company's objective "is to mine, refine, and market silver and precious metals." It was the right time. The price of silver soared to unprecedented heights in the late 1970s and reached an all-time high of

A worker stamps a 100-ounce gold bar with mint mark and weight prior to sale by the Sunshine Mining Company.

$48.07 an ounce on January 22, 1980. But by mid-1982 the price had skidded to $5 an ounce. The price later moved into the $7-to-$8.50 range. The management stockpiled silver, hoping for a better price, and in 1984 looked again to other industries, more particularly oil and gas.

Meanwhile, management consolidated property rights in the Sunshine, and in due course became owner of 98 percent of the mine's production.

The greatest disaster to strike Sunshine was a fire in the mine on May 2, 1972. An unnoticed smoldering fire was fanned into flame by fresh air, and smoke was carried through the entire mine. Herculean efforts were made to rescue the men, and all but ninety-three made it to the surface. Two men were rescued seven days later, but ninety-one perished. A memorial to the men was placed at the mouth of Big Creek.

In an area where air and water pollution are continuing problems, Sunshine serves as a model of environmental awareness. It completed a new 35-acre impoundment pond in 1979 to control water pollution, and it is expected to serve until the end of the century. The company equipped its refineries with a process that virtually eliminates emission of sulfur dioxide into the atmosphere.

Ready-cut potatoes travel on an automated belt line to boxes destined for the McDonald's hamburger chain.

toes and five million pounds of dehydrated onions to government agencies.

After World War II, his major market gone, Simplot turned to research to develop new products for the public. He opened a quick-freeze plant at Caldwell and searched for new uses for the potato in processed form. The frozen french fry was developed along with instant mashed potatoes and innumerable other processed products. By the mid-1980s Simplot had built processing plants in Burley, Heyburn, and Aberdeen, Idaho, in addition to expanding his Caldwell facilities; and in Hermiston, Oregon, and Grand Forks, North Dakota. Simplot supplies millions of pounds of french fries annually to McDonald's, the huge hamburger chain. His potato products are sold in Europe, Japan, Hong Kong, Singapore, and North America.

In 1944, looking ahead to another venture, Simplot was convinced that agriculture must be assured a supply of fertilizers. Southeastern Idaho has one of the nation's largest deposits of phosphate rock, and the Gay Mine, named for his daughter, was opened on the Fort Hall Indian Reservation. Simplot built a plant to process phosphate into fertilizer, and it has operated without halt since. He purchased the Conda Mine of the Anaconda Company in 1960. In 1984 he brought into production the new Smoky Canyon Mine, complete with a 27-mile slurry pipeline to connect with the Conda site, to assure an ample supply of phosphate rock.

The minerals and chemicals division built the Pocatello plant into one of the largest fertilizer processors in the United States. Simplot also has fertilizer plants at Brandon, Manitoba, Canada, and at Helm, El Centro, and Bena, California. Fertilizers are retailed through eighty Soilbuilder outlets in the West and in western Canada.

The division operates a silica mine in Overton, Nevada, and Simplot, with three other investors, purchased the assets of the Bunker Hill Company, near Kellogg, after it was closed.

Simplot's land and livestock divi-

A giant shovel clears overburden on a Smoky Canyon phosphate deposit in southwestern Idaho to supply a Simplot fertilizer plant in Pocatello.

Frozen hash brown potato patties being processed at the J.R. Simplot plant in Hermiston, Oregon.

sion is a model of innovative farming. The division still utilizes unused potatoes and potato waste in feedlots at Caldwell and Grand View, Idaho, at Boardman, Oregon, and at Carberry, Manitoba, Canada. Together these feedlots fatten 300,000 cattle annually. A new system of fattening cattle in confined feedlots was put into operation in the mid-1980s. Less space is required for each animal, and the cattle are monitored by computers. The division also operates dairy and fruit farms in southwestern Idaho, and sells custom-mixed feed rations, animal medicines, and packaged feeds.

The firm has won plaudits and recognition from environmentalists, especially for the restoration work done at the Gay Mine, an open-pit facility, and for water pollution abatement at its plants at Heyburn and Pocatello. It also contributed to air pollution abatement at the Pocatello fertilizer plant.

The J.R. Simplot Company has its headquarters on several floors of One Capital Center, 999 Main Street, a high rise that, along with others, sets off Boise's skyline.

IDAHO STATE UNIVERSITY

Over 10,000 full- and part-time students begin their academic studies each fall at Idaho State University in Pocatello. They benefit from modern facilities in fifty-three major buildings on a 792-acre tract of which 274 are developed and constitute the present campus. They also benefit from a tradition of academic excellence established years ago, from professional administrators, and from friendly and helpful faculty members, two-thirds of whom hold the highest degree offered in their discipline.

On March 11, 1901, Governor Frank W. Hunt signed Senate Bill 53: "An Act to establish and maintain a school to be called The Academy of Idaho at Pocatello." The bill had been drafted and submitted by Senator Theodore F. Turner of Bannock County. Establishment of the academy was contingent upon acquisition of a site that was to be donated by citizens of the community. The land had to be secured by May 1, 1901. Two blocks were donated by Colonel J.M. Ingersoll and two adjoining blocks were purchased for $1,200, and the academy had an 8.5-acre

Looking down from atop Red Hill to the Hutchinson Quadrangle, the heart of the campus.

The upper campus of Idaho State University with the Minidome in the foreground. This was the first covered university arena in the nation.

campus. Immediate plans called for constructing a classroom building and a boys' dormitory. The Main Building, later named Swanson Hall, was completed in time for classes to commence on Monday, September 22, 1902. The dormitory was completed in 1903.

The first Academy of Idaho class consisted of seventy students, fifty-five of whom lived in Pocatello.

They were instructed by four teachers. Courses of study included classical, scientific, and English college preparatory courses and several industrial classes. By 1912 the academy counted 315 students and twenty faculty members, and a campaign was launched to change the status of the school from a college preparatory and industrial arts school to a four-year, degree-granting college. The status and name of the academy were changed, starting with the fall term of 1915. However, the change was to a vocational trade school and a junior college named the Idaho Technical Institute.

In 1927, by direction of the state legislature, the institution was changed to the Southern Branch of the University of Idaho—commonly called the University of Southern Idaho, or the Southern Branch. Academic offerings were expanded as well as intercollegiate activities. Only the pharmacy program was expanded to a three-year course. In 1930 the College of Pharmacy added the fourth year and began awarding the bachelor of science degree. The physical plant expanded despite the stringency of the Great Depression and World War II years.

For some thirty years voices had been raised that a four-year, degree-granting college needed to be established in southern Idaho. That desire was realized when the Southern Branch of the University of Idaho was changed to Idaho State College in 1947. Governor C.A. Robins, using the same pen that had been used by Governor Hunt to create the Academy of Idaho in 1901, signed the legislation affirming the new status of the Pocatello school. A graduate division in education was inaugurated in 1955 and began awarding master's degrees in 1957. The graduate division became the Graduate School in 1967.

The final step in the educational evolutionary process took place in 1963, when Idaho State College was accorded university status by the state legislature. About 6,000 students entered the university in the fall of 1963. Several new colleges were soon added and the curriculum greatly expanded.

University students choose from over 220 fully accredited programs in five colleges and three schools. They can achieve a vocational-technical education or associate, bachelor's, master's, or doctoral degrees.

Looking from the Hutchinson Quadrangle toward the student union building and Red Hill.

While pursuing individual academic goals, each student has access to the Eli M. Oboler University Library, the largest educational building in the state. The library contains well over one million items to facilitate study and research.

The university sports facilities include the Minidome, the first covered university arena in the nation. In 1981 the football team won the national championship in the NCAA

Freshman registration. Over 10,000 students attend Idaho State University on a full- or part-time basis.

division 1AA classification. The Minidome is used for a wide variety of university and community events in addition to athletic contests.

Each student's academic experience may be enhanced by participating in a variety of fine arts and other cultural events and by visiting the Idaho Museum of Natural History on campus. Students from almost every state in the union and several foreign countries interact in social, religious, governmental, or fraternal organizations. Students can relax in the student union, play intramural sports, or pursue a hobby in the mountains or on the rivers in areas near campus.

Because of the university's reputation for academic excellence, a high percentage of graduates are placed in professional positions. Recently the university was listed by the *New York Times Selective Guide to Colleges* as one of the 250 best values in higher education in the United States. Only three other Intermountain West colleges were accorded the same honor. Idaho State University continues to promote excellence in all facets of education.

FALK'S I.D.

Falk is the oldest continuous name in merchandising in Idaho. Falk's I.D., at the corner of Eighth and Main streets in Boise, was until 1982 the oldest store in the same location west of the Mississippi.

The store that Nathan Falk opened in Boise in 1868 expanded into other Idaho communities over the years, and by 1985 Falk's Idaho Department Store was a subsidiary of Interco, Inc., of St. Louis, and operated sixty-nine stores in Idaho, Oregon, Washington, California, Utah, Colorado, South Dakota, and Texas. Its headquarters is in Caldwell, Idaho. Bernard Mayer is president in charge of the Falk's domain.

Boise was only five years old but a permanent settlement with about 400 buildings when Nathan Falk, who had left Bavaria in 1862, opened his dry goods and grocery store on Main Street with the backing of his brother, David. Competition was keen. Idaho's new capital city was the springboard to the rich Boise Basin gold mines, and farming around it was rapidly being developed.

Nathan Falk met the competition from his 25-foot-frontage, two-story building. It was hard work. The store remained open seven days a week and far into the night. Deliveries were made several times a day by wheelbarrow.

During the next twenty years the D. Falk and Bro. store grew as Boise and Idaho grew. A Falk's store was opened in Nampa. The same year Idaho became a state, 1890, the business was incorporated, and it became the Falk-Bloch Mercantile Company.

By 1896 it became necessary to build a new store, and work began at the corner of Eighth and Main streets. Leo J. Falk, Nathan's son, had joined the firm a few years earlier and served as its treasurer. The new three-story building was dedicated in 1897.

Nathan, the store's patriarch, died in 1903, and the following year the store took a new name: Falk Mercantile Company Ltd. Leo Falk purchased additional frontage on Main Street, which ultimately led the way for an expansion in 1928. In 1909 a quality grocery store was established, and H.J. McGirr began his twenty-eight years of service with Falk's.

Falk's celebrated its fiftieth anniversary in 1918, while the nation was at war, and when it was over Ted Falk, another son of Nathan's, joined the firm. The postwar period brought long-awaited prosperity.

The store was expanded into one of the largest emporiums of its kind in Idaho in 1928, and was remodeled throughout. It was the sixtieth anniversary of Falk's service to the community. That same year, 1928, Falk's purchased the Tingwall stores at Caldwell (where the two firms had been joint owners), Fairfield, Wilder,

Nathan Falk, who opened his first store in 1868, presided at the grand opening of this store in 1897.

Jerome, Wendell, Hagerman, Filer, King Hill, and Twin Falls, and the N.K. West and Company store at La Grande, Oregon. In 1943 Falk's celebrated its seventy-fifth anniversary with a party at the Owyhee Hotel. Leo Falk, president of the firm, was also associated with the Owyhee Hotel. Leo died in 1955.

In 1953 the Idaho Department Store group, headquartered at Caldwell, assumed ownership of the Falk Mercantile Company, and it became Falk's I.D. Caldwell continued as the distribution center for the stores of the acquiring company located in southwest Idaho. The purchase of Falk's and the Idaho Department Stores by Interco, Inc., occurred in 1966, and the Falk name was carried on. Falk's I.D. celebrated its 100th anniversary in 1968. Operations in the downtown 1897 store ceased in 1982, but Falk's I.D. had stores in three nearby suburban malls.

CROOKHAM COMPANY

Wherever one buys fresh sweet corn, not only in the United States, but in many parts of the world, it is likely that it grew from hybrid seed husbanded by the Crookham Company of Caldwell.

Since 1931 the firm has been number one in the nation in the production of hybrid sweet corn seed, and 95 percent of all such seed is grown in Treasure Valley. From an immaculate plant, whose specialized machinery was developed primarily by the Crookham Company, about six million pounds of hybrid sweet corn seed yearly is shipped to seed companies nationwide and to Taiwan, Japan, Israel, Mexico, Canada, and Europe.

Crookham spends about one million dollars a year on research, constantly improving hybrid products and plant facilities. While hybrid sweet corn receives its major attention, the company also is number one in the nation in the production of hybrid popcorn seed and of Long day hybrid onion seed. It also produces hybrid carrot seed and lettuce seed.

George Crookham III, son of the founder and now chairman of the board emeritus, has worked with genetics during all his years in the business. He points with pride to the scientists and specialists who head the breeding and research team responsible for the development of the

hybrids. They work, not only with their own nurseries, but also with experimental stations in other states, with seed companies, and with other nations where products from the seed are grown.

The company had 150 sweet corn hybrids in production by 1985, and was concentrating on breeding corn with elevated sugars, known in the trade as "shrunkens." Steve Marshall, who has two doctoral-level degrees and is an acknowledged expert in the field, says that the new hybrids represent a major breakthrough in the popularity of sweet corn.

The hybrids are 80 to 90 percent sweeter than other varieties, and have a shelf life of at least fifteen days. In addition, the shrunkens, so named because they have less bulk than other seeds, can be canned without sugar and salt, an advantage in meeting the dietary needs of the

Three generations of the privately held Crookham Company are (from left) Frank S. Crookham, George Crookham III, George Crookham II, and William Crookham, son of George Crookham III.

world.

The Crookham Company is a family and privately owned corporation, one of the few of its kind in the United States, and has a worldwide reputation. Begun by a pioneer family, it had a hand in the beginnings of the city of Caldwell.

George L. Crookham II married Grace Steunenberg, a sister of Idaho Governor Frank Steunenberg (1897-1905), in Caldwell in 1900, and established his seed business in 1911 featuring popcorn. Sweet corn seed and onion seed were soon added. He sold his business in 1929 to his son, George Crookham III, and a partner who was killed in a plane crash in 1948. Frank Crookham, George's brother, joined the firm in 1931, the year hybrid sweet corn seed production was begun.

George's son, William L. Crookham, joined the firm in 1960 and serves as chairman of the board. Frank Crookham is president.

Not only are the Crookhams preeminent seed producers, they have long engaged in public service, both in the city of Caldwell and at the state level. George Crookham III served four terms in the Idaho legislature, and William served two terms.

The Crookham Company seed plant is located in Caldwell.

NORTHWEST NAZARENE COLLEGE

Northwest Nazarene College, located approximately in the center of the Boise Valley in Nampa, is a recognized liberal arts college in the Christian tradition. The college has sent into the world graduates destined for careers in the Christian ministry, law, business, medicine, teaching, the sciences, engineering, social work, and other professions.

A College of the Church of the Nazarene, NNC had its beginning in 1913, and is looking ahead to its Diamond Jubilee. Northwest Nazarene College has all the attributes of a small private and Church-supported college, especially its commitment to a strong interpersonal relationship between faculty and students. This personalized approach in the instruction of students is not possible in larger universities.

The college's broad mission is geared to its motto, "Seek ye first the Kingdom of God." In brief, its mission and basic purpose is "to develop a Christian perspective on life and to encourage Christian commitment within the philosophy and framework of genuine scholarship." It believes that an education in the liberal arts "enables the student to pursue an understanding of the truth in

study of the scripture, of nature, and of man."

Although a majority of NNC students come from Idaho, Oregon, and Washington, in the 1984-1985 school year they also came from twenty-nine other states and from seven foreign countries. Those of the Nazarene faith dominate on campus, but almost every major denomination of the Christian Church is represented. A number of students are nondenominational.

Faculty members are expected to "pursue excellence of intellectual training, seek integration of faith and learning, and offer guidance toward a world view in both reason and revelation."

The college is governed by a board of regents representing a region of Church support of the institution. The region includes the states of Alaska, Washington, Oregon, Idaho, Montana, and Colorado with parts of Utah and Nevada. Dr. A. Gordon Wetmore, who became the eighth president of the college in 1983, says "Northwest Nazarene College is the story of Christians developing in

Eugene Emerson, founder.

various stages of academic life, and in their preparations for involvement in the realities of life." "Students at NNC," he adds, "understand the Christian discipline of academic excellence."

The college is divided into six academic divisions: fine arts, language and literature, mathematics and natural science, philosophy and religion, professional studies, and social science. The college faculty numbers seventy-five.

Northwest Nazarene College's first classroom and administration building.

The acceptance of the college's graduates for advanced work by top-ranked schools—including the Harvard Medical School, Harvard Law School, Stanford University, University of California at Berkeley, and the Massachusetts Institute of Technology—demonstrates the strength of its academic programs. Further evidence of high quality has been the selection of two of NNC's graduates as Rhodes scholars: John Luik in 1970 and Ginger Rinkenberger in 1984.

NNC makes certain the curriculum keeps up with the times, and with an ever-changing technology. Majors were added in 1983 in computer science and computer information systems. The college has an academic computer center available to all its departments, students, and faculty, and terminals are distributed about the campus.

From its beginning, NNC was recognized for its competence in training teachers. Of the four who graduated in 1917 two were prepared to be teachers. By 1923 one-fourth of the forty-four graduates were teachers. The college was accredited by the state in 1928 as a normal school, and in 1931 as a junior college. It was accredited as a four-year institution in 1937 by the state and the Northwest Association of Higher Education. The following year it was elected to the Association of American Colleges, and additional national accreditations have occurred through the years.

Scholarship standards are high at NNC, but are made easier to attain by the personalized relationship between student and faculty. Religion is a part of student life. Students are required to attend chapel services and convocations, of which there are at least four a week.

There is a bit of everything for students in the college's extracurricular activities. Student organizations are numerous. Intramural athletic activities are available to all. The intercollegiate athletic program includes basketball, baseball, golf, soccer, ten-

Dr. Olive Winchester, vice-president and dean from 1923 to 1935.

nis, track and field, and wrestling for men; and basketball, tennis, track and field, and volleyball for women.

What became Northwest Nazarene College had its beginning in 1913, under the leadership of Eugene Emerson, a Nampa businessman of high integrity who devoted much of his life to the institution. He also served the city as mayor. Emerson provided the land and built a church at the corner of Fifteenth Avenue and Sixth Street South. It was there the school opened for elementary

Dr. Thelma B. Culver, dean from 1946 to 1970.

and secondary students.

A charter for the school was obtained from the state in December 1913, and it granted wide powers to operators of the school. The charter provided "courses of study preparatory for business or professional life or for general culture; to establish classical, mathematical, scientific, technical, theological, agriculture, musical, oratory, physical culture, and general courses of study," and furthermore, "in its theological department, to conserve, maintain, advocate, and promulgate the great New Testament Doctrine of 'Entire Sanctification' or 'Christian Holiness' is the institution committed."

The first college degrees were conferred in 1917. Meanwhile, it became apparent that space was needed for a free-standing school of its own. Mr. and Mrs. Emerson gave ten acres "out in the sagebrush" for a campus, and construction on the new administration building began in the summer of 1915. It was ready for classes at the beginning of the fall term. It measured 120 by 40 feet and had a full basement. The Holiness School became the Northwest Nazarene College in 1916, when sixteen students were enrolled.

The small campus at the end of a dusty road on the outskirts of Nampa, which for a number of years had only three buildings on it, nonetheless attracted students wanting a higher education, and they became fervent alumni of the liberal arts college that gave them the wherewithal to make their way in the world.

From that early beginning the college expanded until in 1985 it had a campus of brick and masonry buildings. By the 1970s the enrollment hovered around the 1,000 mark and reached a peak of 1,352 in 1982.

The history of Northwest Nazarene College is not engraved on its buildings, but comes from the minds, hearts, hands, and faith of a few who left marks never to be erased. They were dedicated to provide for youths, curious and challenged by the future, a Christian education and scholar-

ship in the mold of the Nazarene Church, whose substance created and kept alive Northwest Nazarene College.

It was while Eugene Emerson was in Pasadena, California, that, as a consequence of a religious experience, he felt impressed to establish a holiness school in Nampa. Upon returning to Nampa he worked to help bring the institution into existence, eventually donating land for the first building of the campus. He continued to be an important figure in the success of the college for several years.

John E. Riley served the longest as college president and presided over the greatest expansion of the institution both in buildings and in enrollment. He spent twenty-nine years (1944-1973) on the campus before his retirement, eight as pastor of the College Church, and twenty-one as president. He resided in Nampa after his service.

It was while Dr. Riley was pastor that a new church was built adjacent to the campus. It holds more than 1,000 people and is used as a chapel and convocation auditorium. Most of the major buildings on campus were

erected during his administration, including a number of dormitories, a major classroom building with an education media center, a student union, gymnasium and swimming pool, a science building with a lecture auditorium, and the remodeled old Samaritan Hospital, now a fine arts building. When Dr. Riley be-

Dr. John E. Riley, sixth president, under whose administration the college rapidly expanded in numbers of students, faculty, and buildings.

The John E. Riley Library on the campus of Northwest Nazarene College.

came president, the college had about 450 students and a faculty of 33. When he retired the enrollment was 1,058 students and the faculty numbered 77.

Dr. H. Orton Wiley was president of the college during its formative years. He became president in 1916, the year the school was named Northwest Nazarene College. The institution grew during Dr. Wiley's tenure. He actively solicited funds for the school, and when he was assigned to the Nazarene College in Pasadena in 1926, it had five wooden buildings and had graduated ninety-two students.

One who contributed significantly to the success of the young college's academic development was Olive M. Winchester, who joined the faculty in 1918. She had received her bachelor of arts degree from Radcliff in 1902, and then became the first woman to earn a bachelor of divinity degree from Glasgow University in 1912. After completing a master's degree in sacred theology at Pacific School of Religion in 1917, she came to teach at Northwest Nazarene College. In 1925 she earned a doctorate at Drew Seminary. From 1923 to 1935 she served as vice-president at NNC. Her contribution to the college included helping to establish respect for academic standards and helping to organize the institution.

Dr. Thomas E. Mangum, Jr., a physician who came to Nampa in 1918 to teach prospective missionaries first aid and nursing, established a practice and built a hospital that was associated with the college through its nursing-education program. When Samaritan Hospital closed in 1954 it had graduated more than 200 registered nurses. Dr. Mangum practiced medicine in Nampa for fifty years, and his two sons also became physicians.

Dr. Russell V. DeLong became president of the college in 1927, after Dr. J.G. Morrison served an interim period as head of the institution following Dr. Wiley's assignment to Pasadena. Dr. DeLong was immediately beset with a debt of $93,000. He not only eliminated the debt, he brought about the remodeling of the administration building and construction of a gymnasium. He resigned and returned to New England in 1932.

He was succeeded by Dr. R.E. Gilmore, who served as president during the worst years of the Great Depression, when the college reached a crisis point. Enrollment dropped, as did income from all sources. Faculty divided available payroll monies, and were paid additionally by the trading of services and acceptance of farm produce. The college was threatened with foreclosure for failure to pay $5,000 on a $30,000 note.

Dr. Gilmore resigned in 1935, and Dr. DeLong returned to the college. Highlights of his second presidency were raising money to pay off a considerable part of the indebtedness, winning accreditation of NNC as a senior college, and the construction of Morrison Hall and the R.T. Williams Memorial Library.

Dr. Lewis T. Corlett was named president in 1942, when America's

Dr. Gordon Wetmore became president of Northwest Nazarene College in 1983.

involvement in World War II was a year old. He faced the declining enrollment of young men as they went to war, and lost some of the male faculty. But he made plans for the day when the war would end and the

Dr. Gilbert Ford, longtime professor of physics, became vice-president for academic affairs and academic dean in 1970.

men would return to the campus. It was during the Corlett years that a men's dormitory was constructed. War-surplus buildings, including a mess hall, were moved onto the campus after the war, and the College Church was built during the late 1940s.

During Dr. Corlett's tenure, Dr. Thelma B. Culver became dean of the college; she made a significant mark on the institution from 1946 until she retired in 1970. A graduate of NNC, she was the first to receive her doctorate in education from the University of Colorado in 1947. She reorganized the faculty into divisions. Her work was recognized not only by the Church but by academicians throughout the Northwest. She won numerous honors and memberships in prestigious educational organizations. On her retirement in 1970 she was named dean emeritus for life. Dr. Culver died in March 1984.

Kenneth H. Pearsall, who succeeded Dr. Riley, served during a decade of growing inflation and higher education costs which resulted in financial hardships for many private colleges. Dr. Pearsall worked diligently and managed to keep NNC's enrollment above 1,000. Above all, he had the trust and the support of the constituency in the college's educational zone.

Northwest Nazarene College has the appellation "Crusader" given the student newspaper and the athletic teams. It is an appropriate description of the presidents, the faculty, and the students, who have kept alive the cause, the motto, and the school's mission.

The seventy-fifth anniversary (1988) of the founding of the college will include enlargement of the Endowment Fund to provide increased scholarship offerings and enlarged funding for faculty development. The continuing commitment to value-centered liberal arts higher education places Northwest Nazarene College at the forefront of the cultural development of southwest Idaho.

DIET CENTER, INC.

Sybil Ferguson decided early in 1970 that obesity and malnutrition left a lot to be desired in matters of personal health and pride. She made a firm decision to do something about her situation. What she did was develop a diet that worked for her, then for her friends and neighbors, and then for over four million others. Today people seeking a sensible way to lose weight and maintain that loss need not look far to find a Diet Center. Diet Centers operate in all the states, throughout Canada, and in several other foreign countries.

In 1970, with the encouragement of her husband Roger, Sybil opened her first Diet Center office in a spare bedroom of the family residence in Rexburg, Idaho. She charged a nominal fee as a consultant to those who needed her expertise—gained through personal experience and extensive study of nutrition, disease prevention, and how the body functions. She was soon very busy. By 1972 the idea to franchise the business was ready to be tested. As increasing numbers of people learned that the Diet Center diet was much more than another calorie-counting fad diet, franchises were sold and Diet Centers opened. In 1982 Diet Center was listed sixth out of over 1,300 franchises reviewed by *Entrepreneur: The Business Opportunity Magazine.* Of the numerous fran-

Ferguson Laboratories, a division of Diet Center, Inc., manufactures a full line of vitamins and mineral products as well as a special vitamin supplement that stabilizes dieters' blood sugar levels and eliminates the craving for sweets.

Roger Ferguson, president, and Sybil Ferguson, founder, Diet Center, Inc.

chises dealing with weight control, Diet Center was listed number one. In *Inc: The Magazine for Growing Companies,* December 1983, Diet Center was listed 258th of the 500 fastest-growing American companies.

The genius of the Diet Center program is based upon a nutritious diet and upon a unique counseling program. The diet involves wholesome fresh fruits and vegetables, whole grains, and lean meats. A special vitamin supplement, manufactured in Ferguson Laboratories from natural substances, stabilizes dieters' blood sugar levels and eliminates the craving for sweets—often the downfall of dieters.

The counselors give support to individual dieters on a daily basis during the period that the weight-reduction phase of the diet is in progress. But they do much more than chart the daily weight change of the dieter. All counselors must have lost weight themselves on the Diet Center program and then completed an intensive course at the Dietology School in Rexburg, where they are instructed in the fundamentals of

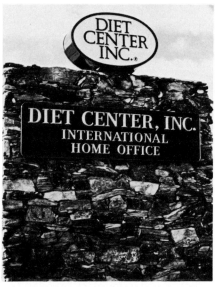

The international home office of Diet Center, Inc., is in Rexburg.

leadership, interpersonal relationships, nutrition, and communication. Each counselor becomes the role model for the dieter, as well as a confidant and friend.

On the logo of Diet Center is the phrase: "How to Win at the Losing Game." Because of the intelligent approach to dieting developed by Sybil Ferguson, coupled with the franchising expertise of Roger, millions of people can identify with that slogan.

TRUS JOIST CORPORATION

The story of Trus Joist Corporation, in capsule, is the marketing of the strongest, lightweight trusses and joists ever conceived in the building industry. They came from the inventive mind of the firm's co-founder, Arthur Troutner. It is a story of Harold Thomas, whose entrepreneurship appears destined to build, in Idaho, one of the nation's largest firms.

Just a quarter-century after its founding in 1960, Trus Joist reached sales over $100 million, and, with a cash flow the envy of any firm, began reaching out for other business opportunities to enhance its standing and its growth.

It all began with Art Troutner, an architect and self-taught engineer. A contractor as well as an architect, he built a number of futuristic buildings in the Boise and Sun Valley area. He became interested in lighter-weight trusses and joists for roofs and floors, and invented an open-web truss that combined wood with webbing of hollow steel tubing. The problem was marketing it.

Then upon the scene came Harold Thomas, a forester, who, in 1959, owned a business selling lumber and glue-laminated beams. Thomas, the salesman, saw the value of the new invention, and a partnership was formed. They opened their business in an old building near the Boise Airport, and in the first year had sales of $49,000.

But the new product, the TJL™

Trus Joist Corporation co-founders Harold Thomas (seated) and Arthur Troutner.

truss, for Trus Joist Light, caught on in the construction industry, and the following year sales reached $285,000. The company moved to a new site on Chinden Boulevard. It built its headquarters there in 1964, and has expanded on that site since then.

In this period Troutner experimented with all-wood joists and trusses, and the result was a lightweight plywood TJI® joist series, a product that consisted of top and bottom flanges of solid-sawn lumber and plywood webs. Then came the development of MICRO=LAM® lumber, a lumber manufactured with

A workman installs TJI® floor joists on a construction job.

veneer running in parallel grain permanently branded under heat and pressure in a continuous process. The advantage of MICRO=LAM lumber is that it can be manufactured in any length without splicing, in widths to forty-eight inches and in depths from three-quarters of an inch to two-and-one-half inches.

Thomas, chairman of the board and chief executive officer, recognized early on that the corporation's proprietary products would command premium prices if sold directly to the end user, and that marketing principle has continued. Walter Minnick, who became president of the corporation in 1979, says the company generates premium prices, "because it produces high-quality products that no other companies have yet matched and markets them direct to the customer." Troutner, who has more than thirty inventions, serves as vice-president, and heads the research and development department.

MICRO=LAM lumber had been found to be especially adaptable to many uses. It is in the electric utility industry as transmission towers, cross arms, and transformer racks. Other uses include concrete forming, highway signposts, furniture frames, bleacher seats, and spars for crop-dusting airplanes.

Trus Joist moved into the international market by entering into a joint venture with Taihei Machinery Works of Japan. The venture provides access to the huge market of Southeast Asia, and to the world's largest supply of hardwood, a veneer that could give MICRO=LAM lumber even more uses.

Trus Joist built new plants in 1984 in Louisiana and Oregon, in addition to thirteen plants in operation in Idaho, Oregon, Colorado, California, Arizona, Georgia, Ohio, and Alberta, Canada. By 1985 the firm had more than 1,400 employees.

TJI® and MICRO=LAM® are registered trademarks of Trus Joist Corporation, Boise, Idaho.

FMC CORPORATION

The history of FMC Corporation's Pocatello plant, which produces elemental phosphorous, began during the Permian geologic age some 200-250 million years ago. During that time the Permian Sea covered most of the future western United States. As the sea withdrew, billions of marine creatures were left behind. Through eons of time their skeletons fossilized and formed huge phosphate shale deposits. The deposits were found near the end of the nineteenth century and were mapped by the United States Geological Survey in 1913. The deposits that supply phosphate shale to FMC's Pocatello plant come from the Gay Mine, an open-pit mine about thirty-five miles northeast of Pocatello on the Fort Hall Indian Reservation. In 1948 FMC leased mineral rights on nearly 7,500 acres of the shale beds from the Shoshone-Bannock tribe.

Prior to 1948 FMC (known as the Food Machinery Corporation since 1929) was involved in such diverse industries as the packing and processing of fresh fruit and vegetables,

A shovel and truck in operation at FMC in 1972.

These specialized railroad cars were used for transporting elemental phosphorous around 1970.

and the manufacture of canning and dried fruit equipment and agricultural pumps and chemicals. The firm also engaged in the development and production of military equipment and defense materials. In 1948 FMC acquired the Westvaco Chemical Corporation and entered the industrial chemical field. The name was changed to Food Machinery and Chemical Corporation at that time. In 1961 the name was changed to the nonrestrictive FMC Corporation.

In 1949 FMC brought its first electric furnace on-line in the Pocatello

plant and produced about 8,000 tons of elemental phosphorous. During that year plans for additional furnaces were announced. Another furnace was started in 1950 and two more in 1952. The capacity of the plant was increased through the years with improved facilities and technology. By 1968 some 125,000 tons of elemental phosphorous was being produced from about two million tons of raw materials—phos-

phate shale, coke, and silica. To produce that amount of phosphorous requires the plant to be in operation twenty-four hours a day, each day of the year, and requires prodigious amounts of raw materials. Five days a week, from sunrise to sunset, April through October, ore is hauled from the Gay Mine to Pocatello in 200 Union Pacific Railroad gondola cars. Each gondola holds 100 tons of ore. A veritable mountain of ore is stockpiled, which will keep the plant in uninterrupted operation from November through March when ore cannot be moved because of weather conditions.

Since elemental phosphorous will ignite if exposed to air, safety requires skilled personnel and specialized equipment. The phosphorous is kept in a liquid state and held under water in storage tanks until transported in specially designed railroad cars where it is covered with water and inert gas so that no air can reach the phosphorus. Shipped to FMC facilities in five states, the phosphorous is converted into phosphates and other phosphorus compounds, which are used in seemingly endless products that affect every facet of our lives. The firm bolsters the economy through its payment of state and local taxes and an annual payroll in the millions of dollars. Additionally, substantial royalties are paid on phosphate ore, and millions of dollars are expended for materials from local suppliers.

FMC is committed to protecting the environment. In the 1970s major equipment and systems were installed to protect the environment and much of that equipment was designed by FMC engineers. When the ore is depleted in one area of the Gay Mine, the pit is back-filled, topsoil is brought in, the land contoured, restored, and revegetated for the grazing of domestic and wild animals.

The employees of Pocatello's FMC facility are proud to be working in the world's largest elemental phosphorous production plant. The aver-

One of the eight fume scrubbers inside the furnace building. These scrubbers help to remove fumes from furnaces that occur during the tapping of slag.

age length of service for almost 600 employees is twelve years, indicating a high degree of job satisfaction. The company offers advancement opportunities in various job classifications. Continuous training is provided to teach new skills or enhance present ones.

About two-thirds of FMC's employees belong to the International Association of Machinists and Aero-

The Pocatello plant of FMC Corporation's Phosphorous Chemicals Division, 1985.

space Workers Union. Management and union work together to ensure good working conditions. Employee involvement is encouraged in standing committees such as safety, communications, benefit association, union management, and others. This provides further cohesion as the employees are involved in creating their working environment.

The firm encourages employees to participate in civic, religious, and service organizations in their communities, and to use their talents to aid youth groups such as Boy Scouts and 4-H. FMC makes annual financial contributions to youth activities, charities, and several other worthwhile community and educational activities. Scholarships are made available for engineering students at Idaho State University, University of Idaho, Washington State University, and Montana State University. Summer jobs in the plant give college students on-the-job training. Employees share their expertise through part-time lecturing and teaching at Idaho State University and other local schools.

No wonder the Chicago-based FMC Corporation is proud of its Pocatello operation. "The men and women that make up FMC Pocatello," noted one observer, "face the future with the confidence of winners."

HECLA MINING COMPANY

Although Hecla Mining Company has interests in at least ten states, the company's origins and heart lie in the silver-rich Coeur d'Alene Mining District of north Idaho. "Hekla" is Icelandic for the verb "to crochet," a word that aptly describes not only the network of tunnels, shafts, and crosscuts honeycombing the Coeur d'Alene District, but also the company's 100-year pursuit of profitable ore through mergers, acquisitions, and joint ventures.

Late in 1883 prospectors rushed to the Coeur d'Alene District in search of gold. Instead they found what was to become the largest silver-, lead-, and zinc-producing region in the nation. The Hecla and Katie May claims became the foundation of Hecla Mining Company, which incorporated in 1891 and began work on a tunnel at the Hecla claim in the town of Burke. Seven years later the firm reincorporated, extended the tunnel, and discovered the main ore body.

By the 1920s the Hecla ore body was decreasing. The company had to expand property holdings, looking first to exploration possibilities into the adjacent Star Mine, owned in part by Bunker Hill and Sullivan Mining and Concentrating Company. The two businesses formed a partnership to develop the mine. Also during the 1920s Hecla purchased holdings in California, Montana, Colorado, and British Columbia.

In 1923 a fire began at the lower end of Burke near the Hecla surface plant and ranged up the confining canyon. All of the town and plant were destroyed. The incident would have spelled the firm's doom were it not for fire insurance and help from other companies in the district. Operations shut down until a new mill was built.

In 1931 Hecla purchased control of Polaris Mining Company and began work on the Polaris Mine near the town of Osburn. Production continued until reserves were exhausted in 1943; however, explorations by Polar-

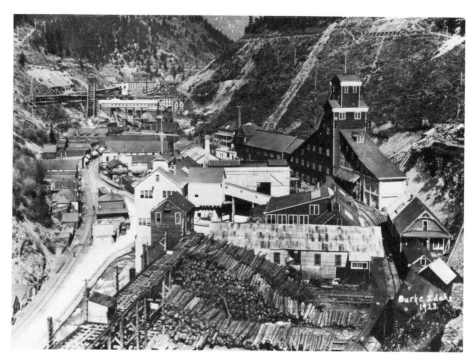

Burke, Idaho, prior to the fire of 1923 that leveled all buildings except concrete structures. The head frame for the Hecla Mine Shaft is to the right. Courtesy, 8-B2 Barnard-Stockbridge Collection, University of Idaho Library, Moscow

is and Sunshine Mining Company revealed a high-grade ore body with years of mining and exploration potential. Hecla and Polaris merged in 1958, giving Hecla control of all Polar-

A workman operates the Long Year, a diamond drill, at the 5,300-foot level of Hecla's Star Mine.

is interests including the Silver Summit Mine.

After 1944 Hecla shut down its original mine. Although World War II boosted prices for lead and zinc, severe labor shortages affected all of the Coeur d'Alene mines. Hecla survived that difficult period by mining and milling a large tonnage of low-grade tailings accumulated on the river flats at Osburn.

After the war and into the 1950s Hecla joined other companies to explore elsewhere in the Coeur d'Alene District. The 1958 purchase of stock in the Lucky Friday-Silver Lead Company proved to be one of Hecla's most profitable ventures. The two companies merged in 1964 and the Lucky Friday Mine near Mullan became the flagship of the Hecla empire.

In 1959 Hecla and Bunker Hill formed the Star-Morning Unit Area. The Morning Mine, which Hecla obtained by lease from Asarco, shares a vein with the Star Mine. It is the largest single lead-zinc vein in the world. The two mines used common shafts and accesses, including tunnel connections to the towns of Burke and Mullan. Hecla and Bunker Hill began extension of a shaft to the 8,100-foot level, 2,344 feet below sea level, to locate deep-seated ore bodies. When the shaft was completed the Star-Morning Mine became the deepest lead-zinc mine in the United States.

Hecla's growth during the 1960s was significant. In 1964 it was listed on the New York Stock Exchange for the first time. By 1966 Hecla maintained exploration offices in Wallace, Reno, Tucson, Salt Lake City, Toronto, and Vancouver, British Columbia. Some ventures were successful, such as Hecla's ten-year affiliation with the Mayflower Mine in Utah, and a cooperative venture with Day Mines. Production from a vein discovered between Day property and the Lucky Friday was split fifty-fifty until the companies merged in 1981. Unfortunately some Hecla ventures were costly failures. Copper mines in British Columbia and Arizona were fraught with problems. Production at Idaho properties helped offset severe losses.

Problems continued into the 1970s. In 1978, to maximize cash flow, Hecla reduced operations at the Wallace corporate office, stopped all exploration outside the Coeur d'Alene District, and closed out-of-state exploration offices. The mining business is never predictable. In 1979 silver prices were up 105 percent. It was

Hecla's Star Mine while in operation in 1980. To the right is the head frame for the mine shaft, shop buildings are in the center, and the mill is in the foreground.

Hecla's best year, with stock on the New York exchange up about 800 percent. Deep exploration was begun at Lucky Friday on a projected 7,700-foot shaft which, when completed, would make it the deepest shaft in the world outside South Africa. In August 1983 the shaft was completed to the 6,205-foot level, with provisions to further extend it when necessary. The Silver Shaft greatly increased Lucky Friday production, making it the largest silver producer in the United States.

Hecla is the largest domestic producer of new silver. Unfortunately, the severe economic recession and low metal prices forced Hecla to shut down the Star-Morning Mine and begin salvage operations, even though the mine was still productive. Hecla also temporarily curtailed production at the Consolidated Silver project, a joint venture to develop properties east of Sunshine Mine through the main shaft of Hecla's Silver Summit. Exploration of the properties continues.

By 1983 prices stabilized and production increased. Hecla was listed

for options trading on the American Stock Exchange. Negotiations with Ranchers Exploration and Development Corporation of New Mexico culminated in a merger in 1984, giving Hecla ownership of the Escalante silver mine in Utah and other Ranchers holdings, including important industrial minerals operations that help to diversify Hecla's income base.

The mining business can reap rich rewards or yield devastating losses. Hecla's 100 years have proven that. However, the fact that the firm has endured is a tribute to the tenacity and determination of Hecla people. Corporate headquarters will be moved to Coeur d'Alene, where transportation and support facilities are more accessible. Nevertheless, the site of principal operations and the headquarters remain in Idaho. It shall continue to be an Idaho business with a future for Idaho.

Underground at the Hecla Mine on December 9, 1906, in Burke, Idaho. Courtesy, 8-X678b Barnard-Stockbridge Collection, University of Idaho Library, Moscow

PRECO, INC.

"Beep-beep-beep." The high-pitched Bac-A-Larm is a familiar sound heard around the world on major equipment. Universally, it indicates that a piece of massive equipment is in reverse. Before Boisean Edwin R. Peterson invented the device, countless lives were lost and injuries sustained when backing vehicles crushed unsuspecting workers.

Peterson is the founder of Preco, Inc., a worldwide electronics manufacturing company and the major producer of the alarms and electronic controls. He is also a born inventor, an auto electrician, and a safety entrepreneur who believes work should be an enjoyable experience.

At first Peterson made his living rebuilding water pumps. A seventy-foot by twenty-foot tin shed on South Sixth Street in Boise served as his original workshop. There were no windows or insulation. For warmth, Peterson jerry-rigged a pot-bellied stove to burn used crank-case oil in a second-hand brake drum.

The first Bac-A-Larm was created in Peterson's basement. In 1968 Preco, Inc., for Peterson Rebuilding Exchange Company, was established with Peterson as owner. Contractors and construction concerns immediately recognized its value, and in due course he was manufacturing the back-up alarm by the hundreds.

Edwin R. Peterson, chairman of the board, with his son, Mark.

A Staten Island, New York, native, he had merited special honors as a captain and pilot during World War II. His inventiveness was put to good use reconstructing damaged Allied aircraft. The Army trained him at Boise's Gowan Field, and after the war he returned to Idaho's capital city.

Preco, Inc., is wholly owned by the Peterson family. Here Edwin Peterson inspects the work at the Boise electronic firm.

By 1975 his business had grown so large that he brought in Jack Y. Robertson as president and chief executive officer. With Robertson's guidance and strategic planning, he propelled Preco into the world's largest manufacturer of back-up alarms with thousands of outlets around the world. By the mid-1980s Preco had expanded its business by manufacturing electronic controls for all types of heavy construction equipment. Contractors discovered their equipment was safer and more productive with the electronic controls.

In 1981 Peterson purchased the Santa Clara Plastics and Manufacturing Company. Due to the keen business sense of Jack Robertson, this once-ailing plastics manufacturing company was turned into a profit-making venture in a short time. The rapid growth of Santa Clara Plastics made it necessary to hire its own division president, and in 1982 Robert Bilow was given command of this post. The firm manufactures what is known in the computer and microchip industries as wet-processing equipment, which is used to etch microchips in acid. The company manufactures numerous models sold to the computer industry worldwide.

By 1985 the two divisions employed over 300 people, and Peterson says the purchase of Santa Clara Plastics resulted in a "good marriage" with his electronic business.

The company is private and family owned, and Peterson plans to keep it that way. His son, Mark, a 1984 electrical engineering graduate, joined the firm that year and is now part of the highly successful team.

Peterson's goal for the decade is to diversify the company's base. He plans to accomplish this task through his New Products Development Division under the direction of Vickie Carruthers. This division will manufacture and market products invented and patented by Peterson during the past several years. "I can't slow up, so I don't know how big one can get, but creating new products is a driving force," says Peterson.

Preco's original facility at Sixth and Myrtle in Boise.

Peterson will be entering the pet, home, and aviation industries with three new products in the near future. Much attention will be devoted to the manufacture, development, and marketing of a dog collar with a retractable leash. He got the idea from his constant standard poodle companion, Gigi. "I was always reaching in my pocket for a leash when I was in a public place, or else I had forgotten it," recalls Peterson, "and I thought there had to be a better way."

The lightweight collar is a simple affair with a nylon leash, complete with a small handle, that retracts into the collar. The collar can be made of any quality material from plastic to diamond-studded leather. Peterson hopes to market it primarily through organizations working with animals, to which would go a portion of the profits.

Peterson believes the retractable-leash concept can be used not only for dog and cat collars, but also for children's harnesses, horses' harnesses, and even for tying a boat to a dock.

In the not-too-distant future is a clock that tells time by tones in var-iables of the note of C. Peterson's conception of a tone clock is exciting. The tones at each quarter-hour are variations of high, middle, and low C, as contrasted to the strikings on a grandfather clock. An automat-

Edwin R. Peterson and chief executive officer, Jack Y. Robertson.

ic volume control is used to make the tones quiet to loud and all degrees between. The tones can be designed for subliminal perception, and in offices and homes can be a constant reminder of the time of day.

Peterson is using his two company aircraft as flying "test beds" for another of his inventions, a simplified electronic aircraft checklist. All items that must be accomplished during the course of any flight are displayed on illuminated push buttons on the checklist. As an item is completed, such as lowering the landing gear before landing, that checklist button is pushed and the light goes out. Any illuminated button reminds the pilot of items that still must be accomplished. In the event of an emergency, the entire checklist can be rotated to bring into view those tasks that must be carried out to safely and efficiently deal with the emergency situation. This inexpensive safety device is extremely versatile and has applications ranging from the smallest general aviation aircraft to the largest commercial transport.

It's all one company, but by the time Edwin R. Peterson reaches the end of his inventive power, it could have a multitude of divisions. Peterson is a man who can't slow up and he looks forward to always working for a "better way" to enjoy life.

THE HOFF COMPANIES, INC.

The name "Hoff" has been part of the history of the lumbering industry in southwestern Idaho for seventy-five years, and it spans four generations in the business.

What Hans and Theodore Hoff started at McCall in 1910, grew through both tribulations and triumphs into what now is Hoff Companies, Inc., and Hoff Timber Company of Boise, devoted to the growth, manufacture, and distribution of forest products. President and chief executive officer is Harvey B. Hoff, great-grandson of Hans Hoff.

The Hoff Companies are family owned, brought to their present state by the hard work and vision of Theodore Hoff, son of Hans, and Theodore Hoff, Jr. Their success is a story of perseverance and belief in the forest-products industry and its people.

Hoff Timber Company, owned by Frances Hoff, widow of Theodore Hoff, Jr., and her children, manages and harvests timber from approximately 10,000 acres of forestland in southwestern Idaho. The timber is sold and delivered to Boise Cascade Corporation mills at Emmett and

Theodore Hoff, Sr. (left), and Theodore Hoff, Jr., inspect a log deck at the Horseshoe Bend mill.

Horseshoe Bend. The latter mill once was the prime Hoff property before it was sold to Boise Cascade.

Hoff Companies, Inc., manufactures and distributes wood products in eastern Oregon, southern Idaho, and Utah. The firm produces lumber

Hans and Theodore Hoff operated the original mill at McCall from 1910 until 1912, when it was destroyed by fire.

for the housing industry at the Hoff Ronde Valley Sawmill in Union, Oregon. About 65 percent of the mill's output is shipped to markets in Boise, Salt Lake City, and Denver. The other 35 percent is exported outside the continental United States, including Japan.

Hoff Companies, Inc., operates molding manufacturing plants at Caldwell and Homedale. The moldings are shipped to southern and eastern markets in the United States. A subsidiary, Trimco, distributes moldings through wholesale outlets in Boise and Salt Lake City. Another subsidiary, Western Forest Products of Boise, distributes wholesale building materials to dealers.

The Hoff building supply centers are retail outlets that serve the communities of Meridian and Weiser, Idaho, and LaGrande and Ontario, Oregon.

Frances Hoff serves as chairperson of Hoff Companies. Officers other than Harvey Hoff are Jim Draper, vice-president of manufacturing; James Kelly, vice-president of finance and controller; and Frank Morrisette, vice-president of marketing. General

Hans Thor Hoff, founder.

offices are at 5440 Franklin Road. The firm employs about 450 people.

Hans Hoff, an émigré from Norway, came to the Pacific Northwest by way of Minnesota, where he married and had a family, of whom Theodore was the first son. Ultimately the two worked together as a team. Theodore married and his first son was named Harvey.

Harvey B. Hoff, right, president and chief executive officer, and Jim Draper, vice-president of manufacturing, view a truckload of molding stock.

Lured by the talk of vast forests in the Northwest, Hans and his wife, and Theodore and his family came to Vancouver, Washington. Theodore found employment with a lumber company and Hans found time to deal in timber.

Two years later—in 1910—the Hoff families moved to McCall, Idaho, and Hans purchased a small sawmill and a flour mill. Improvements were made in the mills and the Hoffs prospered. In 1912 the mills were destroyed by fire. Early the following year Theodore, who had bought out his father, built a new mill and began turning out ties for the railroads, which were expanding their feeder lines, one of them from Nampa to McCall. In 1914, when the railroad reached McCall, Theodore entered into a partnership with Carl Brown, and the firm became known as the Hoff & Brown Tie and Lumber Company. Theodore was recognized as the father of the lumbering business in the Payette Lakes area.

Early in 1929 Theodore sold his interest in the partnership to Brown. He retained a large box factory at Horseshoe Bend, and two cattle ranches near McCall. The forthcoming Great Depression created a stagnant economy in the lumbering business, and the huge box factory was idle. Later it was destoyed by fire.

With the inception of the Civilian Conservation Corps in 1933, the

government enlisted Theodore's help in supervising the work of city-bred men in camps in Idaho's forests. He won citations for his work and served with the CCC until 1938.

After an interlude with a sawmill at Ironsides, Oregon, in which he was joined by Harvey, Theodore returned to Horseshoe Bend in 1941 and purchased a small mill. He was able to finance and expand the mill and it prospered as the Hoff Lumber Company. Harvey had moved to Caldwell and started a lumber and building supply business there.

Theodore Jr., youngest of the family, who served as a Navy pilot in World War II, returned in 1946, and joined his father in the operation of the mill. He brought major changes and expansion to the business. He developed more efficient methods of handling logs, and drying kilns were built. He constructed on the mill site a large plant for the manufacture of moldings and custom mill work, utilizing the latest in automatic and semiautomatic equipment. As a separate operation it became Hoff Forest Products. The complex steadily grew, and by 1967 the two divisions provided primary income for 250 families at Horseshoe Bend. Theodore, who earlier served three terms as a state senator, was honored as Idaho Small Businessman of the Year.

In 1975 the Horseshoe Bend complex was sold to Boise Cascade, and a new firm, Hoff Companies, Inc., was formed with headquarters in Boise. In addition to its forest-products businesses, Ted purchased the Hotel Boise in Boise and began remodeling it into a modern office building, including stores and restaurants. Before it was completed he died of what is commonly known as Lou Gehrig's disease. The Hoff Building later was sold to Idaho Bank & Trust Company.

Harvey Hoff, who had been trained in his father's business at Caldwell and was a rising young executive with Boise Cascade, took over the reins of the Hoff Companies, and the name lives on.

ALBERTSON'S

Joseph A. Albertson is a recognized pioneer in the supermarket industry. He built his first Food Center in 1939 in Boise, then a small city with a population of about 30,000. Forty-five years later Albertson's was the seventh-largest supermarket company and the nineteenth-largest merchandising firm in the United States.

Those who know Joe Albertson are not surprised at his success. He is a gentle but firm person who did not want the spotlight, whose obvious strength and understanding built his merchandising empire.

He began his career as a clerk in a Safeway store in 1927 while still in college at Caldwell, Idaho. He worked his way up at Safeway and early in 1939 decided to go into business on his own, with a one-stop, complete service store rustling in the back of his mind. By 1985, less than fifty years later, Albertson's operates 434 retail outlets in seventeen states extending from near the Canadian border to the Mexican border, and from the Pacific coast of California to the Atlantic coast of Florida, with annual sales approaching five billion dollars.

Joseph A. Albertson, founder.

Albertson opened his first store at Sixteenth and State streets in Boise on July 21, 1939. His partners were L.S. Skaggs, a pioneer drugstore merchandiser, and T.B. Cuthbert. He put $5,000 into the Food Center, and it was, in fact, one of the most modern self-service markets in the country at that time.

Sales for the first six months were $173,272, and the net profit was $9,711. Albertson recalls that his dream was to reach one million dollars in sales in 1940. By the end of 1939 he decided to open a second store at Nampa, and it opened in June of the following year. A third store was opened in November 1940, and the nucleus of a supermarket chain was established. Sales reached $710,000 in 1940, and exceeded the million-dollar mark the following year.

The first store remained in operation in an expanded form until April 7, 1982, when a new superstore was established on what became the four-square-block Albertson's Market Place. Central headquarters for the company, which had been attached to the old store, was moved to a new building at 250 ParkCenter Boulevard on October 1, 1978.

In that first store Albertson had a bakery and made his own ice cream.

Joe Albertson's first supermarket, 1939.

One of Albertson's newest combination food-drug units.

He put in magazine racks, a popcorn machine, and a nut machine. He sold the largest ice cream cone in the area.

During World War II he was faced with keeping food and other items on the shelves. He trucked merchandise from Portland, Oregon, and went through the problems of rationing and food stamps.

The partnership was dissolved in 1945, and Albertson's was incorporated that year. In 1946 sales exceeded $2.7 million, and the profits were $79,636.

By 1959 Albertson's had fifty-one stores. The corporation had a poultry division, a turkey division, a brooder farm, and an egg farm. Albertson's had previously established drugstores, but in 1970 it formed a partnership with Skaggs Drug Stores that was to last until 1977. In 1985 the firm operated ninety combination food-drug units.

The corporation went public in 1959, and its stock is a Wall Street staple. Albertson's continued to build and add stores and in 1974 reached its first one billion dollars in sales. By the end of 1978 it had surpassed two billion dollars, and five years later sales exceeded four billion dollars.

Joe Albertson stepped down as chairman on December 1, 1976, but still serves as chairman of the executive committee. He goes to the office daily, but says, "I let the executives run the company and they are the best in the business." In 1985 the firm employed 35,000 people.

The company's philosophy basically is the same as that propounded by Albertson in his early days. He told the first man ever to interview him for publication that "Merchandising is having goods that customers are ready and willing to buy at prices they are ready and willing to pay, coupled with all the tender, loving care we can give. All of us are human, and being human, we respond to human treatment."

Early on Albertson imbued in his store managers the responsibility of being close to their customers and giving them what they wanted, and that policy has never changed. A section of the firm's corporate philosophy provides that "Albertson's is, in effect, a big store with a specialty store approach. We must be 'big' in terms of low prices, convenience, and wide selection of brands. We must be a 'specialty' store in terms of quality, personal service, and specialized attention."

Albertson's retail operations are organized into four major regions: Intermountain, Northwest, California, and Southern. In 1985 it had in operation eighty-one superstores, ninety combination food-drug units, and 263 conventional supermarkets and other stores.

The supermarkets average about 26,000 square feet, the superstores about 42,000 square feet, and the combination units about 55,000 square feet. The firm operates fully integrated distribution centers in Brea, California; Denver, Colorado; and Salt Lake City, Utah. Produce and limited item warehouses exist in other divisions. A central bakery is situated in Brea, and an ice cream plant is located in Boise.

Albertson's developed one of the most successful private label programs in the industry. Private-label merchandise represents about 20 percent of its total sales.

In 1985 Warren E. McCain, who joined the company in 1952, acts as chairman of the board and chief executive officer. Gary G. Michael is vice-chairman, chief financial officer, and corporate development officer; John B. Carley is president. Executive vice-presidents are Jack Sheehan, retail operations, and Kenneth R. Huff, retail support systems.

H. F. MAGNUSON COMPANY

In 1948, with a borrowed $300, an excellent education from the University of Idaho Southern Branch (ISU) and Harvard Graduate School of Business, and practical work experience at Hecla Mining Company, Harry F. Magnuson opened the accounting firm of H.F. Magnuson & Company in his hometown of Wallace. After taking over an established Wallace accounting firm shortly thereafter, the door was opened to opportunities upon which a man with Magnuson's imagination and determination could capitalize.

His work acquainted him with area businesses, including many of the thirty to forty independently owned mines of Silver Valley. The mining industry, in a decline after the Korean War, was also undergoing a period of retrenchment with many of the original founders passing on. As the mines contracted and several independent operations withdrew, H.F. Magnuson & Company became the central gathering point of many of the firms.

Excellent properties and opportunities became available. When the mining industry boomed in the late 1960s, Magnuson made one sale, of Golconda Mining Corporation stock, at a substantial enough profit to provide "seed money" for its diversification during the next two decades. The company—one of Idaho's largest accounting firms with offices in Wallace, Kellogg, and Coeur d'Alene—acquired in the town of Wallace the Rossi Insurance Company, North Idaho Publishing Company, Stardust Motel, Jameson Restaurant, and a major interest in the First National Bank of Wallace, which has since expanded to ten branches under the name First National Bank of North Idaho.

Diversification also led to property acquisition and land development in north Idaho and eastern Washington, including the University Shopping Center in Spokane, Lewiston Shopping Center, University Inn in Moscow, and a Coeur d'Alene shopping center currently under development.

Harry F. Magnuson. Photograph, Henle-Care Studio

In 1982, when the Bunker Hill Company curtailed operations in Silver Valley, Magnuson formed a partnership with three other prominent Idaho businessmen and purchased the Bunker Hill facilities and mines.

Magnuson, whose roots are firmly planted in Wallace, has always been in the forefront of anything good for the community. Motivated by a desire to preserve Wallace history, he restored Jameson Restaurant and the Rossi Building, founded the Wallace Mining Museum and aided the Sierra Mine Tour. In 1984 he participated on the Steering Committee for Wallace Centennial Celebration. He has also worked to preserve and improve the town's hospital, cemetery, and local newspapers.

In 1984 Magnuson was the recipient of three awards—an honorary Doctor of Law from Gonzaga University, Spokane; the University of Idaho Alumni Hall of Fame Award; and the ISU Businessman of the Year Award. Each acknowledged Magnuson's service to his community, region, and state—a service exemplifying his belief that one who is the beneficiary of success is obligated to give back something in return.

SAFEWAY STORES, INCORPORATED

Few realize that the vast Safeway Corporation, internationally known as a source of excellent goods at moderate prices, began as a small Idaho grocery store.

Safeway's Idaho roots run back to 1915, when Marion Barton Skaggs bought his Baptist-minister father's 18- by 32-foot grocery store in American Falls and began selling to the area's wheat farmers on a cash-and-carry basis, instead of the costly credit system then common among merchants. Skaggs' approach was simple: be content with a small margin of profit, pass the savings along to the customer, and build a high-volume business.

In 1926 Skaggs merged his 428 stores located in ten western states with Sam Seelig's California-based businesses to form Safeway. By 1931, two years after expanding into Canada, Safeway reached its all-time peak of 3,527 retail outlets. During the ensuing decade the total number of stores in the company declined, while the typical store increased in size to accommodate more products and customers. At the same time the firm pioneered such features as free parking to attract customers from a wider area.

The 1940s and 1950s saw many other innovations by Safeway, including the much-imitated "buy-build-sell-lease back" real estate strategy, which provided favorable financing to upgrade the company's store system. Along with introducing significant construction and layout economies, Safeway was also one of the first chains to use interior dec-

M.B. Skaggs' original American Falls store (inset) contrasted with a contemporary Safeway superstore.

orators to plan format and color schemes in its stores for more pleasant shopping.

Safeway is an industry leader in developing programs to help consumers make wise purchase decisions. The company was the first to price produce by the pound, rather than by the piece or bunch. As early as 1935 Safeway was "open dating" products to assure freshness. Safeway also helped pioneer unit pricing to

An old-time Safeway tractor-trailer ready to be loaded.

show both the total price and the price per pound, ounce, or other unit of measurement. In addition, the company moved early and voluntarily to provide essential nutrition information to customers.

During the 1960s Safeway expanded abroad with store operations in Great Britain, West Germany, and Australia. By the mid-1970s Safeway had surpassed A&P to become the world's largest food retailer. With its stock listed on the New York, London, and Pacific stock exchanges, Safeway has traveled far from American Falls. The Baptist minister's son succeeded on a grand scale.

"Distribution Without Waste," the company creed established in the original store, remains the same despite the obvious improvements of today's superstores featuring such amenities as pharmacies, delis, and in-store bakeries.

Today millions of people throughout the United States and around the world shop at Safeway. Every day these consumers can expect to find a vast array of fresh meats and vegetables, dairy products, frozen foods, canned and packaged goods, and other household products—all conveniently located, attractively displayed, and competitively priced.

Patrons

The following individuals, companies, and organizations have made a valuable commitment to the quality of this publication. Windsor Publications and the Idaho State Historical Society gratefully acknowledge their participation in *Idaho: Gem of the Mountains.*

Advanced Input Devices
Albertson's*
Fred L. Andersen
Boise Air Services, Inc.
Boise Cascade Corporation*
Boise State University*
Burley Lions Club
Caldwell Auto Supply
Champion Supply of Boise, Inc.
Crookham Company*
Cummins Intermountain Idaho, Inc.
Dairymen's Creamery Association, Inc.*
Diet Center, Inc.*
Evans Co-Operative Company, Inc.*
Evergreen Ford-Nissan
Falk's I.D.*
Family Medical Clinic
FMC Corporation*
First Interstate Bank of Idaho*
First Security Bank of Idaho*
Friends of Stricker Ranch, Inc.
Gem State Paper & Supply Co.
Dr. and Mrs. Charles G. Hanson
Harmon Travel
Hecla Mining Company*
The Hoff Companies, Inc.*
Idaho Army & Air National Guard
Idaho Bank & Trust Co.*
Idaho First National Bank*
Idaho Forest Industries
Idaho Hospital Association
Idaho Insurance Administrators
Idaho Power Company*
Idaho State University*
Idaho Wine Merchant
Irrigators Lumber Co.
Judi's Bookstore
Lewis-Clark State College*
Floyd Lilly Co.-Dale and Karla Pippitt
Senator James A. McClure
MacGregor Companies*
Magic Valley Library System
H.F. Magnuson Company*
Modern Glass Company
Mountain Bell*

(in memory of) Louisa Murphy
Nelson, Roshott, Robertson, Tolman and Tucker
Northwest Nazarene College*
Optometric Center-Dr. Magwire and Lee
Rick and Sharon Parks
Pillsbury/Green Giant
Pizza Hut of Idaho, Inc.
Preco, Inc.*
Bob Rice Ford Chrysler Plymouth
Robertson's Funeral Chapel, Inc.
Rogers Brothers Seed Company*
Safeway Stores, Incorporated*
Saint Alphonsus Regional Medical Center*
St. Luke's Regional Medical Center*
Shaffer-Buck Agency, Inc.
J.R. Simplot Company*
John W. Spencer
Stapley Engineering
Stellmon Contractors
Stephan, Slavin, Kvanvig & Greenwood
Mr. and Mrs. T.W. Stivers
Mr. and Mrs. Robert K. Stolz, Jr.
Sun Valley*
Sunshine Mining Company*
Symms Fruit Ranch*
The Terteling Company, Inc.*
Treasure Valley Manor
Trus Joist Corporation*
Twin Falls Public Library
United Realty Inc.
University of Idaho*
The Richard H. Waite Family
Waremart Food Centers, Inc.
Robert S. West, M.D.
Western Recycling & Wastepaper Co., Inc.
Willmorth Engineering, P.A.

*Partners in Progress of *Idaho: Gem of the Mountains.* The histories of these companies and organizations appear in Chapter 9, beginning on page 117.

Bibliographical References

Hundreds of articles have been published on Idaho history, primarily in *Idaho Yesterdays* (Idaho State Historical Society) and other Pacific Northwest academic and historical agency quarterlies. Two specialized guides identify all of that literature and include a large number of books issued prior to 1976 and 1979:

Etulain, Richard W., and Swanson, Merwin R. *Idaho History: A Bibliography.* Pocatello: Idaho State University Press, 1979.

Webbert, Charles A., and Nelson, Milo G., eds. *Idaho Local History: A Bibliography with a Checklist of Library Holdings.* Moscow: University Press of Idaho, 1976.

Suggestions for further reading are included in an American Association for State and Local History publication:

Peterson, F. Ross. *Idaho: A Bicentennial History.* New York: W. W. Norton, 1976.

INDIANS AND TRAPPERS

Bird, Annie Laurie. *Old Fort Boise.* Caldwell: Caxton, 1971.

Beal, Merrill D. *"I Will Fight No More Forever"; Chief Joseph and the Nez Perce War.* Seattle: University of Washington Press, 1963.

Bischoff, William N. *The Jesuits in Old Oregon . . . 1840-1940.* Caldwell: Caxton, 1945.

Brown, Jennie B. *Fort Hall and the Oregon Trail.* Caldwell: Caxton, 1932.

Drury, Clifford M. *Chief Lawyer of the Nez Perce Indians, 1796-1876.* Glendale: Arthur A. Clark, 1979.

_____. *Diaries and Letters of Henry H. Spalding and Asa Bowen Smith Relating to the Nez Perce Mission, 1838-1842.* Glendale: Arthur H. Clark, 1958.

_____. *Henry Harmon Spalding.* Caldwell: Caxton, 1936.

Haines, Francis. *The Nez Perces: Tribesmen of the Columbia Plateau.* Norman: University of Oklahoma Press, 1955.

Josephy, Alvin M. *The Nez Perce Indians and the Opening of the Northwest.* New Haven: Yale University Press, 1965.

_____. *Nez Perce Country.* Washington: National Park Service, 1983.

Liljeblad, Sven. *Indian Peoples in Idaho.* Pocatello: Idaho State College, 1957.

_____. *Idaho Indians in Transition, 1805-1860.* Pocatello: Idaho State University Museum, 1972.

Madsen, Brigham D. *The Lemhi: Sacajawea's People.* Caldwell: Caxton, 1979.

_____. *The Northern Shoshoni.*

Caldwell: Caxton, 1980.

McDermott, John D. *Forlorn Hope: The Battle of Whitebird Canyon and the Beginning of the Nez Perce War.* Boise: Idaho State Historical Society, 1978.

Schoenberg, Wilfred P. *Paths to the Northwest: A Jesuit History of the Oregon Province.* Chicago: Loyola University Press, 1982.

Slickpoo, Allen P. *Noon Nee Me Poo (We, the Nez Perces).* Lapwai: Nez Perce Tribe of Idaho, 1972.

Walker, Deward E. *Conflict and Schism in Nez Perce Acculturation: A Study of Religion and Politics.* Pullman: Washington State University Press, 1968.

_____. *Indians of Idaho.* Moscow: University Press of Idaho, 1978.

MINERS

Fahey, John. *The Ballyhoo Bonanza.* Seattle: University of Washington Press, 1971.

_____. *The Days of the Hercules.* Moscow: University Press of Idaho, 1978.

Magnuson, Richard G. *Coeur d'Alene Diary: The First Ten Years of Hardrock Mining in North Idaho.* Portland: Metropolitan Press, 1968.

Grover, David H. *Debaters and Dyna-*

Boise-Payette Lumber Company was formed in 1923, and this view of a retail outlet in Cascade was taken soon after. The company was a forerunner of Boise-Cascade. (ISHS)

miters: *The Story of the Haywood Trial.* Corvallis: Oregon State University Press, 1964.

Little, Dallas E. Livingston. *An Economic History of North Idaho, 1800-1900.* Los Angeles: Journal of the West, 1965.

Smith, Robert Wayne. *The Coeur d'Alene Mining War of 1892.* Corvallis: Oregon State College, 1961.

FARMERS AND RANCHERS
Arrington, Leonard. *Beet Sugar in the West: A History of the Utah-Idaho Sugar Company, 1891-1966.*

_____. *Great Basin Kingdom: An Economic History of the Latter-day Saints, 1830-1900.* Cambridge: Harvard University Press, 1958.

Bachman, J. R. *Story of the Amalgamated Sugar Company.* Caldwell: Caxton, 1962.

Burcaw, G. Ellis., and Ehrenreich, Dixie, eds. *Rural Life in the Palouse.* Moscow: University of Idaho Museum, 1982.

Davis, James W., and Stillwell, Nikki Balch. *Aristocrat in Burlap: a History of the Potato in Idaho.* Boise: Idaho Potato Commission, 1975.

Davis, Nelle Portrey. *Stump Ranch Pioneer.* New York: Dodd, Mead and Company, 1942.

Elsonsohn, M. Alfreda E. *Pioneer Days in Idaho County.* 2 v. Caldwell: Caxton, 1947-1951.

Foote, Mary Hallock. *The Chosen Valley.* Boston: Houghton, Mifflin and Company, 1902.

_____. *The Desert and Sown.* Boston: Houghton, Mifflin and Company, 1892.

Greenwood, Annie Pike. *. . . We Sagebrush Folks.* New York: D. Appleton Century, 1934.

Jordan, Grace. *Home Below Hell's Canyon.* Lincoln: University of Nebraska Press, 1954, 1962.

McEwen, Inez Puckett. *So This is Ranching.* Caldwell: Caxton, 1948.

Meinig, Donald William. *The Great Columbia Plain; a Historical Geography, 1805-1910.* Seattle: University of Washington Press, 1968.

Ourada, Patricia K. *Migrant Workers in Idaho.* Boise: Boise State University, 1980.

Rockwell, Irving E. *The Saga of American Falls Dam.* New York: Hobson Book Press, 1947.

Smythe, William Ellsworth. *The Conquest of Arid America.* New York: Harper, 1900.

Yost, George, and d'Easum, Dick. *Idaho: The Fruitful Land.* Boise: Syms York, 1980.

LOGGERS
Hidy, Ralph W. *Timber and Men: The Weyerhaeuser Story.* New York: Macmillan, 1963.

Hult, Ruby El. *Northwest Disaster; Avalanche and Fire.* Portland: Binfords and Mort, 1960.

Jordan, Grace. *The King's Pines of Idaho: A Story of the Browns of McCall.* Portland: Binfords and Mort, 1961.

Little, John J. "The 1910 Forest Fires in Montana and Idaho; Their Impact on Federal and State Legislation." Master's thesis, University of Montana, 1968.

Space, Ralph S. *The Clearwater Story: A History of the Clearwater National Forest.* Missoula: United States Forest Service, 1964.

Spencer, Betty G. *The Big Blowup.* Caldwell: Caxton, 1956.

TRANSPORTATION
Athearn, Robert G. *Union Pacific Country.* Chicago: Rand McNally, 1971.

Beal, M. D. *Intermountain Railroads: Standard and Narrow Gauge.* Caldwell: Caxton, 1962.

Hult, Ruby El. *Steamboats in the Timber.* Caldwell: Caxton, 1968.

Hedges, James B. *Henry Villard and the Railways of the Northwest.* New Haven: Yale University Press, 1930.

Jackson, W. Turrentine. *Wells Fargo and Co. in Idaho Territory.* Boise: Idaho

Permeal French grew up and taught school in the mining camps. She became the first woman elected to public office in Idaho in 1898 when she served as state superintendent of public instruction. She later became dean of women at the University of Idaho. (ISHS)

The Craig Mountain Lumber Company locomotive pushed ponderosa pine logs near Winchester in the last decade of steam railroading. Henry R. Griffiths, Jr., recorded the scene in 1946. Courtesy, Henry R. Griffiths, Jr.

State Historical Society, 1984.
White, Wayne E. *A History of Aviation in Idaho*. Boise: Boise State University

CITIES AND TOWNS
BLISS:
Gentry, James R. *A Centennial History of Bliss, Idaho, 1883-1983*. Bliss: Centennial Committee, 1983.

BOISE:
Eggers, Robert F. "A History of Theater in Boise, Idaho, from 1863 to 1983." Master's thesis, University of Oregon, 1963.

Hart, Arthur. *Fighting Fire on the Frontier*. Boise: Fire Department Association, 1976.

Wells, Merle. *Boise: An Illustrated History*. Woodland Hills, California: Windsor Publications, 1982.

BUHL:
Byrne, Lloyd E. *Buhl "As It Was."* Boise: Syms-York, 1976.

BRUNEAU:
Jones, George R. *Bruneau As I Knew It, 1912-1945*. Boise: Syms-York, 1963.

CALDWELL:
Hall, William W. *The Small College Talks Back*. New York: Richard R. Smith, 1951.

CASTLEFORD:
Early History of Castleford, Idaho. Castleford: Community Men's Club, 1974.

CHESTERFIELD:
Lavina Fielding Anderson, ed. *Chesterfield: Mormon Outpost in Idaho*. Bancroft: Chesterfield Foundation, 1982.

Diffendaffer, Marguerite Moore. *Council Valley: Here They Labored*. Council: Worthwhile Club, 1977.

DECLO:
Clayville, Margaret, ed. *Declo: My Town, My People*. Declo: History Committee, 1974.

DIXIE:
Sweeney, Marian S. *Gold at Dixie Gulch*. Kamiah: Clearwater Valley Publishing Company, 1982.

EMMETT:
Lyon, Ruth B. *The Village That Grew*.

Boise: Lithocraft, 1979.

GIBBONSVILLE:
Randolph, Julia, compiler. *Gibbonsville, Idaho: The Golden Years*. Gibbonsville: Gibbonsville Improvement Association, 1982.

GOODING:
Buckway, JaNene Johnson. *Good Beginnings*. Gooding: Chamber of Commerce, 1983.

GRACE:
Simmons, Vivian, and Varley, Ruth. *"Gems" of Our Valley*. Grace: Grace Literary Club, 1977.

LEWISTON:
Hibbard, Don. *Normal Hill: "An Historic and Pictorial Guide."* Lewiston: Luna House Historical Society, 1978.

LEWISVILLE:
Lindstrom, Joyce. *Lewisville Centennial, 1882-1982*. Rexburg: Ricks College Press, 1982.

MACKAY:
Olson, Georgia Perdue. *Mackay's Yesterdays*. Arco: Arco Advertiser, 1978.

MIDDLETON:
Foote, Morris. *One Hundred Years in Middleton*. Middleton: Boise Valley Herald, 1963.

MOSCOW:
David, Homer. *Moscow at the Turn of the Century*. Moscow: Latah County Historical Society, 1979.

Gibbs, Rafe. *Beacon for Mountain and Plain*: Story of the University of Idaho. Moscow: University of Idaho, 1962.

NAMPA:
Bird, Annie Laurie. *My Home Town*. Caldwell: Caxton, 1968.

PARIS:
Arrington, Leonard. *Charles C. Rich: Mormon General and Frontiersman*. Provo: Brigham Young University Press, 1974.

Reitzes, Lisa B. *Paris: A Look at Idaho Architecture*. Boise: Idaho State Historical Society, 1981.

Rich, Russel R. *Land of the Sky-blue Water: A History of the LDS Settlement of Bear Lake Valley*. Provo: Brigham Young University Press, 1963.

PARMA:
Lowell, Helen, and Peterson, Lucille.
Our First Hundred Years: A Biography of Lower Boise Valley. Caldwell: Caxton, 1976.

POCATELLO:
Gittins, H. Leigh. *Pocatello Portrait: The Early Years, 1878-1928*. Moscow: University Press of Idaho, 1983.

Kissane, Leedice. *Pocatello Memories: A Collection of Columns from the Idaho State Journal*. Pocatello: Idaho State University Press, 1983.

Beal, Merrill D. *History of Idaho State College*. Pocatello: Idaho State College, 1952.

PRESTON:
Hart, Newell. *Hometown Sketchbook: Preston's Main Street in Transition*. Preston: Cache Valley Newsletter Publishing Company. 1981.

REXBURG:
Crowder, David L. *Rexburg, Idaho: The First Hundred Years, 1883-1983*. Caldwell: Caxton, 1983.

RIGBY:
Scott, Patricia Lyn. *The Hub of Eastern Idaho: A History of Rigby, Idaho, 1885-1976*. City of Rigby, 1976.

SILVER CITY:

Adams, Mildretta. *Historic Silver City: The Story of the Owyhees*. Homedale: Owyhee Press, 1960, 1969.

Chadwick, Alta Grete. *Tales of Silver City*. Boise: Boise Printing Company, 1975.

Welch, Julia Conway. *Gold Town to Ghost Town: The Story of Silver City, Idaho*. Moscow: University Press of Idaho, 1982.

SUN VALLEY:
Oppenheimer, Doug, and Poore, Jim. *Sun Valley: A Biography*. Boise: Beatty Books, 1976.

Taylor, Dorice. *Sun Valley*. Sun Valley: Ex Libris Sun Valley, 1980.

TWIN FALLS:
Wright, Patricia. *Twin Falls Country: A Look at Idaho Architecture*. Boise: Idaho State Historical Society, 1979.

WEISER:
Hibbard, Don. *Weiser: A Look at Idaho Architecture*. Boise: Idaho State Historical Society, 1978.

WESTON:
Fredrickson, Lars. *History of Weston, Idaho*. Logan: Utah State University Press, 1972.

These rough old boys were photographed by pioneer photographer William Henry Jackson at Sawtell Ranch at Henry's Lake in 1872. Courtesy, National Archives

249

Index